CONTENTS

PREFACE

Many of my colleagues in Wisconsin have covered the Green Bay Packers far longer than I have. And perhaps they've seen players come farther than Aaron Rodgers has.

But in my 15 years covering the Packers, Rodgers improved more than anyone I've witnessed.

When Rodgers arrived in the spring of 2005, he was lost. Inaccurate. Overwhelmed. Frustrated.

But one thing Rodgers never lacked was confidence.

No matter how bad he looked—and there were times it wasn't pretty—he never doubted himself. Today, we know why.

Rodgers is smiling last, and smiling the widest, after leading the Packers to a championship in Super Bowl XLV, and winning NFL Most Valuable Player awards in both 2011 and 2014.

Rodgers had a postseason for the ages in 2010 and became just the 29th quarterback to ever win a Super Bowl title. Rodgers joined Bart Starr and Brett Favre as the only Packers' signal-callers to win Super Bowls. And he thrust himself into a discussion of the NFL's best quarterback.

It was a remarkable transformation for a player that struggled immensely that first summer in Green Bay. Back then, Rodgers' delivery was mechanical. He didn't appear to have the athleticism he now possesses. And his arm strength, a major positive today, appeared only so-so back then.

Anyone that tells you they would have bet on Rodgers becoming a star is probably fibbing. There were no signs of it that first summer.

But Rodgers is as sharp as they come. He's bright, witty, and articulate. In fact, there are many days Rodgers will challenge the media as much as they challenge him.

So it was simply a matter of time before he grasped things mentally. What came as a surprise is how much he improved the other aspects of his game.

By Rodgers' second summer in Green Bay, he was a different player. By his third, he looked like starting material.

In fact, after Green Bay lost the 2007 NFC Championship Game to the New York Giants, one Packers assistant coach told me that many on the staff believed they would have defeated the Giants if Rodgers—not Favre—had been the quarterback that night.

Emboldened by that belief in Rodgers, it was easier for Green Bay to let Favre retire, then eventually trade him in the summer of 2008. Still, that lengthy soap opera made Rodgers a nationwide talking point.

While Rodgers' development as a player was significant by that time, his growth as a person came out in that crazy summer.

Each day, Rodgers was bombarded by questions about Favre, as well as his own future. What did Rodgers think about Favre wanting to return? Could he live with being a backup again? Did he still want to be in Green Bay? The questions were endless.

Rodgers was 24 years old at the time, and many people that age would have been overwhelmed. Instead, Rodgers stayed the course and bit his tongue. He came off as professional and classy. And he may have won

AARON RODGERS

TITLETOWN MVP

ROB
REISCHEL

This book is available in quantity at special discounts for your group or organization.
For further information contact:

Triumph Books LLC
814 North Franklin Street
Chicago, Illinois, 60610
Phone: (312) 337-0747
www.triumphbooks.com

Printed in the United States of America
ISBN: 978-1-62937-242-6

Editorial production and layout by Alex Lubertozzi

Photos on pages 15, 16, 17, 18, 19, and 35
© 2015 by Chico Enterprise-Record, reprinted with permission.

Photos on pages 3, 31, 33, and 39 © 2015 by Jim Biever, reprinted with permission.

All other photos courtesy of AP Images unless otherwise indicated.

For Laura, Maddie, and Mia—the best team in town

more points for his behavior in that ordeal than any touchdown pass he's ever thrown.

Twelve months after the Favre saga, Rodgers and I sat together inside Lambeau Field shortly before training camp opened. We discussed football, life, and Favre.

"I think I earned a lot of fans nationally, who maybe didn't know me or know a lot about me, by handling things the way I did," Rodgers said. "It was a difficult situation, but I just tried to be as honest and as classy as I possibly could. I realized the situation was way bigger than myself, and I think in doing that, I earned the respect of my teammates, the organization, and our fans. And I think people that didn't know me nationally took notice, too."

They haven't stopped.

The Packers went just 6–10 that first year under Rodgers, but have risen since. First, there was a playoff appearance in 2009. Then, with expectations sky high in 2010, the Packers survived a glut of injuries and became Super Bowl champions.

Green Bay reached the playoffs six straight years between 2009 and 2014 and won four straight NFC North titles from 2011 to 2014. Entering the 2015 campaign, Rodgers was 70–33 as a starter (.680), ranks No. 1 in NFL history in passer rating (106.0), and had thrown 226 touchdowns and just 57 interceptions.

Rodgers' ascension to NFL MVP is one of the league's most compelling stories in recent memory. Remember, Rodgers had zero NCAA Division I scholarship offers coming out of high school, he plummeted down draft boards in April 2005, and he was forced to wait three years for his chance in Green Bay.

At every turn, Rodgers has faced long odds. Each time, he's succeeded.

"The guy has overcome a ton," teammate Jordy Nelson said. "A ton."

The next challenge will be for Rodgers to keep improving and help the Packers win multiple Super Bowls in the years ahead.

Back in the summer of 2005, I wouldn't have thought it possible that Rodgers would one day lead Green Bay to a Super Bowl. I was dead wrong.

You'll never catch me betting against him again.

—Rob Reischel

Aaron Rodgers looks for a receiver downfield during the Packers' Week 2 victory over the Seattle Sawhawks in Green Bay on September 20, 2015.

1

A DREAM COME TRUE

Aaron Rodgers ducked under center Scott Wells, took the final snap of the 2010 season, and touched his left knee to the ground. Rodgers put the ball in his left hand, took off his helmet, and was then embraced by teammates from every angle. As confetti fell from Cowboys Stadium like snow on a Wisconsin winter day, Rodgers made his way to a football-shaped podium in the center of the field. There, America's newest "Golden Boy" hoisted the Vince Lombardi Trophy and was given his signature title belt by teammate Clay Matthews.

The Green Bay Packers were NFL champions once again, following their thrilling 31–25 win over Pittsburgh in the Super Bowl XLV. And Rodgers—who was named the game's Most Valuable Player—was the biggest reason why Green Bay could be called Titletown once again.

"It is a dream come true," Rodgers said that night. "It's what I dreamt about as a little kid watching Joe Montana and Steve Young, and we just won the Super Bowl."

Rodgers had just finished a Super Bowl performance—and a playoff run—that rivaled any the NFL has ever seen. He carved up a Pittsburgh defense that was allowing an NFL-best 14.5 points per game by throwing three touchdown passes and completing 24-of-39 passes for 304 yards. He then joined Bart Starr as the only quarterbacks in Packers history to be named MVP of a Super Bowl. That capped a memorable postseason in which Rodgers threw for 1,094 yards and nine touchdown passes in four games. The only quarterback prior to Rodgers to throw for more than 1,000 yards and nine TDs in one postseason was Kurt Warner.

Rodgers led the Packers to three road wins and helped Green Bay become the first No. 6 seed from the NFC to ever reach a Super Bowl. Then, Packers head coach Mike McCarthy put the entire offense on Rodgers' shoulders in the title game, and he was the No. 1 reason Green Bay defeated the vaunted Steelers. Thanks to one magical postseason run, the names Brady, Manning, and Brees were no longer alone when discussing the NFL's top quarterback. Rodgers was now part of the discussion.

"I think it tells the world that Aaron is for real," Wells said afterward. "There were a lot of questions this postseason coming from the exterior, outside of our own locker room. We always had confidence in him and what he's been able to do. He's our guy, we love him, and I think this man has silenced some of the doubters out there."

Rodgers has faced doubters every step of his remarkable journey. And it could be argued that of the 31 quarterbacks that have won Super Bowls, Rodgers overcame the most obstacles and longest odds to reach football's pinnacle. Undersized in high school, Rodgers didn't receive a single NCAA Division I scholarship offer. He went the junior college route, before University of California coach Jeff Tedford discovered him.

Aaron Rodgers is all smiles during player introductions before a 2010 preseason scrimmage. And why not—the Packers were being picked by many as the favorite to win it all.

"IT'S WHAT I DREAMT ABOUT AS A LITTLE KID WATCHING JOE MONTANA AND STEVE YOUNG.

—Aaron Rodgers

Rodgers waited, waited, and waited some more during the 2005 NFL Draft before the Packers finally took him with the 24th overall pick. Then Rodgers played the waiting game for three years while he sat behind Packers icon Brett Favre.

"He has had a hard road for no reason," Packers wideout Jordy Nelson said. "He was behind Brett. Give him credit for learning and not just sitting there and waiting for Brett to be done. He went about and perfected his game. He stepped up, and you see where we are now."

It's unlikely the Packers would have been in this position had they caved in to the indecisive Favre during the wild, wacky summer of 2008. Favre had retired that March, then changed his mind and wanted to return. But the Packers believed they had something special with Rodgers and made the controversial move of trading Favre, a sure-fire, first-ballot Hall of Famer. Three years later, Rodgers made general manager Ted Thompson and head coach Mike McCarthy look like geniuses when he vanquished the ghost of Favre.

"I've never felt like there's been a monkey on my back," Rodgers said. "The organization stood behind me, believed in me. I told Ted back in 2005 he wouldn't be sorry with this pick. I told him in '08 that I was going to repay their trust and get us this opportunity."

As unlikely as Rodgers' story is, the tale of the 2010 Green Bay Packers was equally improbable.

Ravaged by injuries unlike any Green Bay team in more than three decades, the 2010 Packers were a constant work in progress. By the time the regular season ended, 15 players had gone to the injured reserve list, and eight of those started at least one game.

"We've had some adversity," Matthews said. "We've had to fight through it all season. We had some key contributors go down. The young guys stepped up. The playmakers on this team continued to take their game to a whole other level."

There were plenty of potholes, though. Green Bay lost consecutive overtime games in mid-October and found itself a disappointing 3–3. But a four-game winning streak—highlighted by a pair of victories over Favre and the Minnesota Vikings—got the season steered back in the right direction.

Just when it appeared Green Bay had battled through its injury woes, Rodgers suffered a concussion in the second quarter of a Week 14 game in Detroit. Rodgers missed the rest of that game and the following week in New England. The Packers lost both of those contests and were just 8–6 with two games remaining.

"Those last couple of games of the regular season, we had to win those games," cornerback Charles Woodson said. "It felt like a playoff game for us."

And Green Bay played that way, too. Rodgers had arguably the finest performance of his career during a 45–17 destruction of the visiting New York Giants. Then in the regular season finale, Rodgers and the Packers rallied past a Chicago team trying to knock Green Bay out of the postseason. The Packers were into the tournament, but they had to do something no NFC team had ever accomplished: reach the Super Bowl as a No. 6 seed.

Green Bay quarterback Aaron Rodgers, shown scrambling from danger during Super Bowl XLV, had the entire offense placed on his shoulders that night—and delivered.

"We always believe. We know who we are," said linebacker Desmond Bishop, Rodgers' teammate at Cal. "We know the talent we have on this team. And, we just had to figure out a way to put it all together. When we won our last two games, it all clicked. Relentless pursuit of perfection and we found greatness."

They sure did, and so did their 27-year-old quarterback.

A quarterback's reputation is built by what he does in the playoffs, and that's why Rodgers' stock was sky high following the 2010 postseason.

First, he led the Packers to three straight road wins to capture the NFC Championship. Then, Green Bay knocked off a Pittsburgh team that had won two of the last four Super Bowls. Suddenly, talk of Rodgers not being able to win a big game seemed laughable.

"One thing, that guy is a true leader," wideout Donald Driver said. "He goes out week in and week out and proves people wrong. He proved it once again, and he can now say that he is one of the best quarterbacks in this game."

There would be few arguments after what Rodgers did in the 2010 postseason.

First, he carved up a Philadelphia defense by throwing three TDs and outplaying Michael Vick during a Wild Card win over the Eagles. It was Green Bay's first playoff win ever in Philadelphia. Then it was on to Atlanta where Rodgers had a performance for the ages. Three TD passes. A ridiculous passer rating of 136.8. A completion percentage of 86.1 percent. And zero Packers punts. Green Bay trampled the NFC's top seed 48–21, and Rodgers was becoming one of football's hottest names.

(above) Pittsburgh's defense came into Super Bowl XLV ranked first in the NFL in points allowed (14.5), but Aaron Rodgers and the Packers erupted for 31 points against the vaunted Steelers. (opposite) Packers quarterback Aaron Rodgers celebrates after throwing a first-half touchdown in Super Bowl XLV. Rodgers threw three touchdowns and no interceptions in the game.

Pittsburgh linebacker James Harrison is one of football's fiercest players. Despite relentless pressure, Aaron Rodgers stood in against Harrison and the Steelers' pass rush and led the Packers to victory.

"It's an unbelievable feeling," said rookie cornerback Sam Shields, who had two interceptions against the Bears, including one in the closing moments. "There are a lot of guys that waited a long, long time for this."

Rodgers' wait to reach football's grandest stage wasn't necessarily lengthy, but it was filled with far more questions than most Super Bowl quarterbacks are ever presented. Would a scholarship offer ever come around? Why did 21 teams—including Dallas and Minnesota twice—pass on Rodgers during the 2005 NFL Draft? Would Favre ever leave? And finally, could Rodgers adequately replace one of the greatest quarterbacks in NFL history and win over a fan base?

"I think he's a very mature young man," Thompson said of Rodgers. "In some ways sitting for three years and then playing is helpful. That's the way it was back in the day. You always brought quarterbacks in, and you developed them for about two or three years before you actually played them. That's hard to do anymore. I think that was helpful. He was able to sit back, watch, listen, and learn. Like I said, he's a very good quarterback, and I think the best is yet to come."

Thompson was right. The best came in the 45th Super Bowl, where Rodgers had the weight of the offense on his shoulders and delivered with an unforgettable night.

"He is the reason they won," Steelers defensive lineman Brett Kiesel said of Rodgers.

Indeed. Never forget, this was football's best defense Rodgers was dissecting. The Steelers simply didn't allow teams to run the ball. And if you became one-dimensional, Pittsburgh pass rushers like James Harrison and LaMarr Woodley began licking their chops.

Rodgers never blinked, though. He made quick decisions, was remarkably accurate, and showed courage against the rush as Green Bay threw the ball on 39 of its 52 offensive plays (75 percent).

"He played a great game," Packers left tackle Chad Clifton said. "He made a lot of plays out there today from inside the pocket and outside the pocket. He is a phenomenal quarterback."

"He was on fire," Packers coach Mike McCarthy said of Rodgers. "He likes playing in domes, and you can see why."

Rodgers and Green Bay's offense weren't as sharp during a 21–14 win over Chicago in the NFC Championship Game. But the Packers were good enough to beat their oldest rival in the 182nd—and most important—meeting in this remarkable series.

For the first time in 13 years, Green Bay had won the NFC and would play for an NFL championship.

Green Bay Packers quarterback Aaron Rodgers was named the Most Valuable Player of Super Bowl XLV. Rodgers joined Bart Starr and Desmond Howard as the only Packers to earn that honor.

Afterward, the Packers were NFL champions for a league-high 13th time. And Rodgers was not only a Super Bowl champion, but an MVP as well. Every question had been answered. His wait was officially over.

"It's a special honor to be one of the leaders of this football team," Rodgers said. "I've said it once, and I'll say it again: no one person has ever won a game by themselves. This is a team effort and a great group of men. Special guys, and I'm just blessed to be one of the leaders on this team.

"Individually, it's the top of the mountain in my sport, my profession. It's what you dream about as a kid and think about in high school, junior college, D-I: getting this opportunity and what would you do? I'm fortunate and blessed to play for a team that believes in us. At the same time, I wanted to make sure I was the most prepared guy on the field to have this type of performance."

Rodgers most certainly was. In many ways, though, he had been preparing his whole life. ■

2

THE PRIDE OF CHICO, CALIFORNIA

Football was always king to Aaron Rodgers. From his days at Whitford Middle School in Beaverton, Oregon, through a terrific career at Pleasant Valley High School in Chico, California, Rodgers always dreamed about playing in the NFL. He lived and died with the home state San Francisco 49ers. He even wore a Joe Montana T-shirt under his uniform as he got older.

Just one problem: when Rodgers entered high school, he was a scrawny 5′2″, 130 pounds.

"He was little," said Ron Souza, Rodgers' quarterbacks coach at Pleasant Valley. "But he was very gifted for a little guy. He had excellent mechanics and always had a great understanding of football. Watching film, his readiness to learn, the whole mental part he was terrific at. And then he started growing."

Rodgers, the middle of three boys, was a late bloomer. By the time his senior season started, though, he was 6′, 180 pounds and still growing.

Rodgers lit it up his last two years at Pleasant Valley, throwing for more than 4,400 total yards during his junior and senior seasons combined. He also set school records for touchdown passes in a game (six), all-purpose yards (440), and twice was an all-section choice.

But Rodgers was far from a household name. And Chico, located 90 miles north of Sacramento, is hidden away in the Northern Sacramento Valley. So when Rodgers' senior season ended, not a single Division I school offered him a scholarship.

"We just don't get a lot of exposure up there because maybe a lot of the coaches and players don't understand how to get the most exposure for your players," Rodgers said. "For me, I didn't go to any Nike camps, didn't get my name out there.

"We're north of Sacramento, and we just don't produce a lot of top athletes. You look at my high school team, and we had three guys who went on to play football...so it's not like we've got a hot-bed of Division I athletes over there. So a lot of times when one does come along they get overlooked."

Rodgers, a terrific student, thought long and hard about giving up football—and going to college as strictly a student.

"There was a time I thought about that, for sure," Rodgers said. "I had finished my senior year of football, I wasn't playing basketball. It was January, and I was working out and stuff and meeting with a couple of coaches. The reality was sinking in that, 'Hey, you're not going to get a scholarship.' So now I had some choices to make."

But Craig Rigsbee, the head coach at nearby Butte College back then and its athletics director today, threw Rodgers a lifeline. And today, all of Packer Nation should be grateful.

Aaron Rodgers was undersized at Pleasant Valley High School and didn't receive a single NCAA Division I scholarship offer.

Chico Enterprise-Record/Bill Husa

Chico Enterprise-Record/Glenn Fuentes

Chico Enterprise-Record/Glenn Fuentes

Rigsbee had watched Rodgers in a passing league the previous summer and liked what he saw. Butte, a junior college of 5,600 full-time students, was located just 15 miles outside of Chico. Rigsbee had turned the Roadrunners into a national power and thought Rodgers could be his next great quarterback.

There was just one problem: Darla Rodgers.

"I lived one cul-de-sac away from his family, so in January [of Rodgers' senior year] I walked over there one night," Rigsbee said. "Right away his mom, Darla, said, 'No kid of mine is going to a J.C.'"

You can see why Darla Rodgers felt that way. Aaron Rodgers had a 3.5 grade-point average, extremely high test scores, and could certainly qualify at many high-level academic institutions.

But as Rigsbee continued talking, the Rodgers family became believers.

"Initially, my Mom didn't want me there," Rodgers said of Butte College. "My Dad had gone to a few Butte games, and it was a wild bunch. So she didn't think that was a good spot for me. But Coach Rigsbee is like a big brother still. He's one of the greatest guys I know. He's done so much for so many guys at Butte College. Once he came over, he's a heck of a recruiter. It was a no-brainer. That's where I wanted to go.

"I remember one question that kind of sealed it for me. I said, 'Coach, if I have one good year, would you be willing to allow me to leave? And he said, 'For sure. I don't want to get in the way of you fulfilling your dreams. But you've got to win the starting job first.' So I went out there and won the job."

Butte had a returning quarterback named Brian Botts who was in his third year with the program. Botts

(top left) Rodgers was clocked in the low 90s while pitching for Pleasant Valley High School in 2002. (bottom left) Aaron Rodgers has a laugh with his parents, Ed and Darla Rogers. (top right) After high school, Rodgers spent a year at Butte College in Chico, California.

had paid his dues, and most figured he would play in front of Rodgers. Rigsbee was extremely impressed with both players during practices that summer. But Rigsbee kept coming back to one play, more than any other.

"By the time [Aaron] got to us, he had grown another inch and was maybe 195," Rigsbee said. "And on about the second day of practice, he threw a 50-yard dart back to the left. I turned to my assistants and said, 'Did you guys just see that?'"

Still, not everyone was convinced. At the end of camp, Rigsbee solicited the opinions of his assistant coaches on what to do at quarterback.

"Every guy on the staff said they'd go with [Botts]," Rigsbee said. "Finally I said, 'This is why I'm the head coach. We're going with Aaron.' The kid had been here two weeks, and he was already better than the kid that was here three years. And I said after a game or two, he's going to be 100 times better."

Rodgers faced an uphill battle to become the starting quarterback at Butte College. But once he did, he led the Roadrunners to a 10–1 record and a No. 2 national ranking.

Chico Enterprise-Record/Bill Husa

Rigsbee had also promised Rodgers he would do everything possible to help him land a Division I scholarship after one season. So that October, Rigsbee arranged for University of California coach Jeff Tedford to attend practice. It's been widely reported that Tedford came that day to see Butte tight end Garrett Cross, who eventually went to Cal. That wasn't the case, though.

"He was there to see Aaron," Rigsbee said. "And it was kind of a wild practice. We were throwing on every play and running 7-on-7 drills. I mean, we never ran 7-on-7s on Mondays, so guys were wondering what was going on. At the end of practice, Tedford came over to me and said, 'He's the best junior college quarterback I've ever seen.' And I just said, 'Right on!'"

Right on indeed, as Tedford offered Rodgers a scholarship that day.

"Seeing him in person, he was very impressive," Tedford said. "He was very accurate, threw the ball well, and had a tight spiral. It was a very pleasant surprise to find out he was very strong in other categories as well."

Rodgers immediately showed that at Cal, too. He didn't win the starting job in fall camp in 2003, but he had claimed the position by Week 5. Rodgers led the Golden Bears to a 7–3 mark in their final 10 games and threw for 2,903 yards and 19 TDs. Rodgers, who's extremely protective of the ball, had streaks of 98 and 105 consecutive passes without an interception. He led the Bears to late-season wins against Washington and Stanford to clinch a berth in the Insight Bowl. Then

Botts left the program after two games. Rodgers led the Roadrunners to a 10–1 record, a No. 2 national ranking, and a NorCal Conference championship. Rodgers threw for more than 2,400 yards, 28 TDs, and just four interceptions. Perhaps most importantly, though, Rodgers learned how to lead.

"That was the most important year of my young football career," Rodgers said. "I learned a lot about myself that year, being an 18-year-old playing with guys from all over the country and different countries: Canadians, a 25-year-old center, guys who had been to prison, guys who had been bounce-backs from Division I, local guys, and trying to be an 18-year-old and lead those guys and figure out a way to lead them. I learned a lot about leadership and a lot about myself, and I also got my confidence back because I had a real good season, so that was an important year. I still keep in touch with a lot of those guys and my coach as well."

Rodgers was discovered by University of California coach Jeff Tedford, who told Butte College coach Craig Rigsbee, "He's the best junior college quarterback I've ever seen."

Rodgers threw for 394 yards and was named MVP in Cal's bowl win over Virginia Tech.

Rodgers was even better the following year, when he guided the second-highest scoring offense in school history. Rodgers threw for 2,566 yards and 24 TDs, with just eight interceptions, and was named first-team all–Pacific 10.

After Rodgers' junior season, NFL scouts gave him a first-round grade, and many believed he would be taken extremely early in the draft. So he declared for the NFL Draft with one year of eligibility left. It was quite a journey for a player who couldn't get a glance from college recruiters just three years earlier.

"Recruiters put so much into height and weight," Rodgers said. "I was a little under what I am now, and my area doesn't get heavily recruited, either. I'll tell you what: I'm a firm believer that everything happens for a reason."

In the weeks ahead, that philosophy would most certainly be put to the test. ∎

In two years at California, Rodgers threw for more than 5,400 yards and 43 touchdowns.

COMBINE HIGHS, DRAFT-DAY LOWS

Aaron Rodgers was one of the stars of the 2005 NFL Combine. Bright, articulate, personable, Rodgers was a hit almost everywhere he went. One night, Rodgers sat down with members of the Green Bay Packers front office. But with the Packers slated to pick at No. 24 in two months, both sides figured they wouldn't see each other again.

"I remember telling them 'Trade up. I'd love to play for you guys,'" Rodgers recalled. "And they were saying, 'Well, you probably won't be available when we want to get you.'"

It was easy to think that way. Rodgers had enjoyed remarkable success at the University of California. In two seasons as a starter, Rodgers threw 43 touchdowns, 13 interceptions, and for nearly 5,500 yards. Rodgers had shown outstanding accuracy, evidenced by his 23 straight completions against USC, which tied an NCAA record. He also scored an impressive 35 on the 50-question Wonderlic test.

"I think I'm a student of the game," Rodgers said that February. "I think I pick up an offense pretty quickly. Prepare for a game, just watch a lot of film, know your opponent as well as knowing your own team and your strength. For me, it was tough this year because we lost a lot of receivers, so I had to continually work in practice to get the timing down with those guys. Just constant film study and the mental preparation, I think. Visualizing good plays in your mind so when it comes game time

you've already seen yourself do that in your mind already, and it just becomes second nature, muscle memory."

On the flip side, the 6′2″ Rodgers was at least an inch shorter than many teams wanted at the position. Although he weighed 223 pounds, it was clear he still needed to add bulk. But the biggest question Rodgers answered that week was about his delivery and playing for Cal coach Jeff Tedford.

Tedford turned the likes of David Carr, Kyle Boller, Trent Dilfer, Akili Smith, and Joey Harrington into college standouts and first-round NFL draft picks. But none matched that success at the next level. Green Bay general manager Ted Thompson remembers asking Rodgers about that very topic during their 15-minute get-together at the Combine.

"We actually asked Aaron in our interview at Indy about that," Thompson said. "He says he's better than all of those guys, so we feel pretty good about that."

Darrell Bevell, who was Green Bay's quarterbacks coach at the time, remembered the exchange, as well.

"It's kind of a tense atmosphere in that room," Bevell said. "You've got a young man [Rodgers] sitting there, you've got...some pretty heavy hitters talking to him. You're really trying to get the questions that you want to get through, so you're kind of just taking it in. But I was impressed with him a little bit. I kind of like him to have a little bit of a chip on his shoulder and want to prove those critics wrong."

Aaron Rodgers, shown here running the 40-yard dash at the 2005 NFL Combine, was projected to be one of the top picks in that year's draft.

Rodgers seemed to win people over with his intelligence, confidence, and quick wit. And when Rodgers left Indianapolis that February, many expected San Francisco to make either him or University of Utah quarterback Alex Smith the No. 1 pick. The debate intensified even more after both had sublime workouts on their pro day.

Smith received a standing ovation after his performance. Rodgers didn't get quite as much love, but he certainly impressed.

"Alex is a great player," Rodgers said. "It's funny because my first big game was his first big game. His first start was my first extended playing period at Cal, so I kind of followed his career from then. He's a little taller than I am, I think. We both put up some good numbers this year. I'm just excited about going up against him, being able to run against him, throw against him, and see how we stack up."

That decision eventually would be made by San Francisco head coach Mike Nolan, who was given total autonomy with the No. 1 pick. And Rodgers was hopeful he'd made a lasting impression on Nolan—and the rest of the NFL brass at the Combine.

"As time has gone on the last month or so, to me, I'm very confident there's going to be a guy who fits," Nolan said.

Indeed there was. Rodgers just didn't like who it was.

April 23, 2005, was supposed to be the best day of Aaron Rodgers' young life.

Rodgers was holding out hope that his home-state team—the San Francisco 49ers—would use the No. 1 pick in the NFL Draft on him. Even if that didn't happen, Rodgers figured to go early that day. Instead, Rodgers' stay inside the "Green Room" at the Jacob K. Javits Convention Center in New York City was almost hard to watch.

"Well, obviously when you're sitting in the green room, you just want to get out of there," Rodgers said.

It took until the 24th pick that excruciating day before Rodgers heard his name called. That's when the Green Bay Packers threw Rodgers a net and broke his fall.

"Did we think he was going to be there when we were watching tape? No," Thompson said. "But over the course of the last week or so there was a couple of, I don't know, websites, or ESPN, or something that said maybe he might get there. So, I went back and did a little more work just to make sure. But I feel very comfortable that this kid warranted being picked where we were at."

Just a few weeks earlier, it seemed incomprehensible that Rodgers would be around at pick No. 24. At one point, the 49ers were negotiating with representatives for Alex Smith, wideout Braylon Edwards, and Rodgers about becoming the draft's top pick. When the 49ers decided on Smith, though, it sent Rodgers into a free fall.

Only Cleveland, Tennessee, and Arizona were teams with top 10 picks that had a possible need at quarterback, and when they went in different directions, Rodgers kept spiraling. There were a couple more chances for Rodgers to find a landing spot inside the

Fans Steve Tate, left, and Dan Kursevski look over possible picks during a Lambeau Field Atrium draft party on April 23, 2005.

top 15. That didn't happen, though, and when Houston passed at No. 16, a string of teams with proven quarterbacks also went in different directions.

Green Bay was another team that appeared set at quarterback. But with Favre aging and always unsure about his future plans, Thompson selected the highest remaining player on his board.

"When it got past 16 (Houston), we knew the teams at 17–23 probably weren't going to take me, and Green Bay was probably our next option," Rodgers said on draft day. "And the more I thought about it the more I realized it could be a great fit for me, being able to learn from one of the best quarterbacks of all time and to not be thrown in the fire right away and to come to a team with a storied franchise and a winning tradition. I think it's going to be exciting. It's going to be a great fit."

In Thompson's mind, he had gotten a steal. The Packers had Rodgers ranked far higher than No. 24 on their draft board. Green Bay also felt Rodgers was entering an ideal situation, one where he could watch

Aaron Rodgers, joined by fellow draft prospects Cedric Benson, left, and Antrel Rolle, center, attempts to throw a ball through a tire during a New York television appearance prior to the 2005 NFL Draft.

"I KIND OF LIKE HIM TO HAVE A LITTLE BIT OF A CHIP ON HIS SHOULDER AND WANT TO PROVE THOSE CRITICS WRONG."

—Darrell Bevell

across as too cocky during pre-draft interviews. Perhaps, but most teams also want a high level of confidence and self-assuredness from that position. What might have hurt Rodgers more than anything was the brutal track record of Tedford-coached quarterbacks. Several NFL executives simply figured Rodgers was next in line to flop.

The Packers most certainly didn't share that belief, though.

"If there was a report that he was going to slip I would have been shocked," Bevell said. "I'm still in a little bit of a state of shock that he came down to us, and it's an exciting pick for us."

Tedford's quarterbacks were often called robotic, and because of their deliveries, they couldn't translate their collegiate success to the NFL. When Rodgers stepped out from under center as a collegian, he immediately brought the ball up near his earhole, which is about a foot higher than someone like Favre, who held the ball at shoulder length. The advantage to Rodgers' delivery was that the release is short and compact so he could get rid of the ball quickly. The drawback is that Rodgers didn't bring the ball back as far as other quarterbacks, so his strength on deeper passes was affected.

On draft day, Rodgers indicated he'd rather not mess with his throwing motion but said he'd adjust if told to.

"I'm very coachable, so if the coaching staff here wants me to think about changing that up, I'll definitely be open to doing that," he said. "But unless I find a

and learn in a low-pressure environment. Then when Favre did eventually leave, Rodgers would have had ample time to prepare.

"I'm sure it was a long day for Aaron," Cal coach Jeff Tedford said on draft day. "People thought he would be one of the first five picks, and it didn't work that way. A lot of teams didn't need quarterbacks. But if I know Aaron, he will take this as motivation. He's going to have talent around him, and there's not a better guy to learn the game from than Brett Favre."

At the end of the day, no one could determine exactly why Rodgers had plummeted that day. Some NFL personnel people later said Rodgers had come

Aaron Rodgers plummeted to the 24th overall pick in the 2005 NFL Draft before the Green Bay Packers broke his fall. (opposite) Rodgers acknowledges cheers from the audience after the Packers made him their first selection in the 2005 NFL Draft.

Todd Blackledge, and Art Schlichter) were complete busts.

So, based on 20 years of history, the odds of Rodgers hitting it big were roughly 30 percent.

"I didn't know that, but now I'm all depressed," Thompson said. "I don't know. I think a lot of times the urgency to get a quarterback and the importance of that position and plus there are so many things going on that make up a really good quarterback...sometimes there's not that much difference between a really good quarterback and one that can't quite function amongst the chaos that happens once you snap the ball. I don't think you know that until you really have it. I think most of the quarterbacks who come from the first or the second round, sometimes from the sixth round as we know with Tom Brady, clearly it's not an exact science, but you try to make the best judgments you can. I haven't really thought about the failure or the success rate of the first-round quarterback."

Thompson certainly started thinking about it more that night, after making Rodgers his first-ever pick as Green Bay's general manager. Rodgers, on the other hand, was just happy his long day had ended.

"I noticed looking at my watch a couple of times and hours were passing," he said. "We got excited a few times hoping that teams were going to take a chance on me. I got some calls from some friends, and I just tried to stay positive knowing that God had a plan for me where I didn't see where his hand was at the time, but now I know that he has had this plan for me since the beginning of time, and I'm excited to be a Packer."

The excitement was just beginning. ■

different way of throwing, I don't really feel like the way I throw is a negative. But I'm definitely open to suggestions."

As Rodgers entered the league, he did so at a position that faced long odds. Between 1982 and 2001 there were 37 quarterbacks taken in round one. By subjective count, 11 of those (Michael Vick, Donovan McNabb, Daunte Culpepper, Peyton Manning, Steve McNair, Drew Bledsoe, Troy Aikman, John Elway, Jim Kelly, Dan Marino, and Vinny Testaverde) proved more than worthy of their draft status. Another 11 (Bernie Kosar, Kerry Collins, Trent Dilfer, Chad Pennington, Chris Miller, Jim Harbaugh, Jim Everett, Tony Eason, Ken O'Brien, Jim McMahon, and Tommy Maddox) were solid pros. Finally, 15 others (Tim Couch, Akili Smith, Cade McNown, Ryan Leaf, Jim Druckenmiller, Heath Shuler, Rick Mirer, David Klingler, Todd Marinovich, Jeff George, Andre Ware, Kelly Stouffer, Chuck Long,

(above) Aaron Rodgers celebrates with his mother, Darla, and father, Ed, after being drafted by the Green Bay Packers. (opposite) Aaron Rodgers holds up a Green Bay No. 1 jersey on draft day 2005. Little did anyone know that by Rodgers' sixth season, he and the Packers would be No. 1.

THE UNDERSTUDY YEARS

When Aaron Rodgers arrived at Butte College back in the fall of 2002, he asked to wear No. 12, his old high school number. That was already taken, though, by a player named Shaun Bodiford who, ironically, Rodgers would later play with in Green Bay. Rodgers then asked for No. 8 because his boyhood hero, Steve Young, wore that number. But that was taken, too. Rodgers finally asked Butte coach Craig Rigsbee for No. 4. Why? "He told me, 'I just love how Brett Favre plays,'" Rigsbee said. "Pretty ironic." That's for sure.

Now, Favre and Rodgers were teammates, and things didn't get off to a stellar start. Rodgers arrived in Green Bay for his first mini-camp less than a week after he was drafted and immediately found himself in the middle of a firestorm. During an interview with ESPN, Rodgers was asked his thoughts on Favre being given the camp off. His response? "Lazy," Rodgers quipped. While Rodgers' tongue was firmly planted in his cheek, some took the brash rookie's comment the wrong way.

At the time, Favre had started 205 consecutive games in Green Bay, a streak that would reach 253 by the time he left. And while Rodgers insisted he was joking, he immediately knew it was a bad joke.

"That was a joke. It was definitely a joke," Rodgers said the next day. "Bad sense of humor. Brett's a phenomenal quarterback, and I just hope he didn't take it the wrong way because I was simply joking."

The relationship between Favre and Rodgers got off on the wrong foot, and it remained icy throughout. Rodgers simply wanted to learn from one of the NFL's best. But Favre viewed Rodgers as a threat and hated the fact that the Packers had his eventual replacement in house. Favre had no desire to tutor Rodgers. Instead, Favre was doing all he could to hang on.

During that first mini-camp, though, Rodgers showed he had miles to travel before becoming Favre's successor. The pinpoint accuracy and confidence he displayed at Cal were gone. Far too many of Rodgers' throws sailed high on him. And he was indecisive in his reads. Even though Rodgers' struggles were par for the rookie course, the Packers seemed concerned.

"Something is causing him to have his ball sail," offensive coordinator Tom Rossley said of Rodgers. "He's high on all of his throws. He's not really cutting loose, and he's not following through and finishing on the ball. I want to see him torque and throw the ball hard. I think then the ball will start coming out at a better trajectory."

After his first mini-camp, Rodgers admitted he was extremely overwhelmed.

"I did throw a lot of high balls," Rodgers said that weekend. "I've always said you throw from the ground up, from your feet up. And when you're not confident in your reads, you're late on stuff, you rush stuff, your feet are out of position, and the ball goes high. And until I

The relationship between Aaron Rodgers and Brett Favre got off to a rough start and never got much better.

> ## "HIS MECHANICS ARE (EXPLETIVE) UP. EVERYTHING HE THREW AT CAL WAS DINK AND DUNK STUFF. I SAW HIM THIS SUMMER, AND HE STUNK THE PLACE UP."
> ### —AFC scouting director

get my timing down on these plays, I will throw some high balls. My IQ's pretty high, and I am picking it up pretty fast. I think the coaches would say that as well. As far as calling the plays, that's getting better and better every day I'm getting better at that. I don't feel I'm playing terrible. But obviously I want to get better, and I'm excited about doing that."

It didn't happen for Rodgers that summer, either. During Rodgers' first training camp, he quarterbacked Green Bay's offense for 20 series against No. 2 and 3 defenses. On just one of those did Rodgers lead the Packers to any points. Throughout that summer, Rodgers won points for his pocket awareness, nifty feet, and terrific poise, which helped him survive behind a makeshift offensive line. Rodgers also showed more athleticism than many thought he possessed coming out of Cal. But too often, Rodgers settled for checkdowns instead of looking downfield.

The scouts that doubted Rodgers on draft day had even more questions now. They wondered if Rodgers had an NFL-caliber arm. They questioned if Rodgers' big numbers at Cal came largely from the quarterback-friendly system employed by Jeff Tedford. And ultimately, many doubted if he could someday replace Favre.

"I was never a Rodgers guy from the start," one AFC college scouting director said before the 2005 season began. "His mechanics are (expletive) up. Everything he threw at Cal was dink and dunk stuff. I saw him this summer, and he stunk the place up."

When summer ended, many wondered if Rodgers deserved the No. 2 spot instead of veteran Craig Nall. The previous season, Nall had posted a lights-out passer rating of 139.4 while occasionally relieving Favre.

But when the regular season began, Rodgers was named No. 2. And while the move may have been political, Rodgers did all he could to prove it was the right choice.

"I'm just starting to climb to my potential," Rodgers insisted. "I feel real confident, and I'm making good steps. I'm getting better each day. I feel more confident, more comfortable in the pocket and in this offense. Obviously, we've got to execute a little better and make some plays when we get the opportunity. I've got to put the ball in better spots, but I felt good about making plays outside the pocket when the pocket broke down. And I just think I'm going to keep getting better."

Rodgers didn't change a lot of minds during the regular season, though. The 2005 campaign was a miserable one in Green Bay. The Packers were ravaged by injury, began the year 0–4, and were just 2–10 in early December. Favre was struggling through a brutal season, one in which he'd eventually throw 29 interceptions and just 20 touchdowns. Many fans began clamoring for Rodgers, to see if a few months of watching had helped the No. 1 draft pick.

But Mike Sherman, who was stripped of his general manager duties the previous offseason and would

try to win every game you play, and if you don't try to win every game you play, then you're in the wrong business. You're here to win. I think Brett's playing as good as he's ever played. He's still one of the best quarterbacks in this league, and he makes plays that no other player can make. If you're going to put your best player on the bench, I don't know what kind of sense that makes. I think it's insane to even bring it up."

So Rodgers' rookie season ended like it began: with a whimper. He relieved Favre in three games and went 9-of-16 for 65 yards. Rodgers didn't throw a touchdown, had one interception, and put up a paltry quarterback rating of 39.8. One season in, Rodgers was still being billed as the heir apparent to Favre. His play, though, didn't exactly win anybody over.

be fired as head coach after the season, had no interest in what Rodgers could do. Remember, Sherman never wanted Rodgers in the first place. He wanted some help for a leaky defense or a new offensive weapon for Favre. The last thing Sherman wanted general manager Ted Thompson to do was draft a quarterback to sit on the bench.

So when the Packers bottomed out that year, Sherman certainly wasn't going to turn things over to a player he didn't want in the first place.

"I can't see not playing to win a game," Sherman said. "I think that's what we're supposed to do. We're going to play to win."

Considering Rodgers had shown very little at that point, the Packers themselves certainly weren't arguing.

"I'm just going to put it to you this way," veteran right tackle Mark Tauscher said. "(Favre's) a great quarterback. I don't think there's been any slip in his game, his play has kept us competitive, and he's done everything in his power to make this team win. So why would you take away your best weapon and put in someone with no experience and so much youth?

"There's time to develop guys, and times to try and win games. You don't develop guys to win games. You

So after Green Bay's dreadful season had concluded, the Packers were all crossing their fingers that Favre would come back in 2006 and Rodgers could continue developing.

"I think Aaron will be fine when he gets his chance," wideout Donald Driver said that year. "Now hopefully, he doesn't get that chance for a while. The

(top) Facing constant media scrutiny, Aaron Rodgers struggled immensely during his first mini-camp and first training camp in Green Bay. (bottom) Brett Favre had a rough 2005 season, but the Packers never gave serious consideration to sitting him and playing Aaron Rodgers.

best thing that could happen is for Brett to come back, because that man still has a lot of football in him. Then Aaron could keep learning and be even more prepared when his chance comes along."

. . . .

The 2006 offseason was a tumultuous one in tiny Green Bay. Sherman was fired one day after the Packers' season finale. Ten days later, Mike McCarthy—who was San Francisco's offensive coordinator when the 49ers passed on Rodgers—was hired as the 14th head coach in Green Bay history. And after Jeff Jagodzinski was brought in as offensive coordinator and Tom Clements was hired to coach quarterbacks, Rodgers was suddenly working with an entirely new coaching staff.

Whereas Sherman and his staff had elected not to mess with Rodgers' carriage, McCarthy's staff slowly tinkered with his release point. Instead of that mechanical motion where Rodgers was throwing the ball from the ear hole of his helmet, McCarthy gradually lowered the delivery. Suddenly, Rodgers' throwing motion looked more natural and effortless.

From the start of training camp that summer, Rodgers was a different player. Some of it had to do with his improved delivery. But much of it was the simple fact that Rodgers now understood his playbook from A to Z. Instead of thinking, Rodgers was simply playing football again.

"He's comfortable and that's the whole thing," wideout Donald Driver said. "When you're comfortable in the offense, it makes it easier to just go and play. He's more comfortable and more relaxed and much better than he was last year."

That showed throughout Rodgers' breakthrough summer. Rodgers finished the preseason with a quarterback rating of 101.1 and led Green Bay's No. 2 offense to 24 points in 22 possessions. A year earlier, Rodgers had a paltry quarterback rating of 53.0 in the preseason.

"I think it went a lot better," Rodgers said of his 2006 preseason. "We put some points on the board. Overall, I think it was a good experience, and I got a lot better. The offseason work definitely paid off. We'll see how it goes."

In four preseason games, Rodgers completed 22 of 38 passes (57.9 percent) for 323 yards. He threw three touchdowns, had one interception, averaged 8.5 yards per pass attempt, and lost two fumbles. In the 22 series Rodgers conducted, he led the Packers to 25 first downs, and Green Bay averaged 5.0 net yards per play.

A year earlier, Rodgers was 20-of-37 (54.1 percent) for 172 yards, an average of just 4.65 yards per passing attempt. He threw two interceptions, one touchdown, and was admittedly lost at times.

"What's the difference between this year and last year?" Rodgers asked. "Comfort level, knowledge of the offense, confidence. I feel like I'm a much better player than I was last year. Obviously, that won't bear a lot of fruit until I have a chance to be a starter, but I feel good about where I'm at after preseason camp No. 2."

Rodgers was generally more consistent in practice each day, as well. In 11-on-11 drills, he completed 165 of 263 passes (62.7 percent) with seven interceptions. In 7-on-7 drills, he was 102-of- 159 (64.2 percent) with two picks.

"He's getting better," Packers coach Mike McCarthy said of Rodgers. "You're looking at a guy who's going to mature. He's got athletic ability that people still haven't seen. He's confident and has a really good understanding of what's going on. I just think from the film I watched last year, he's really improved. He has a chance to be a really good player."

Rodgers also showed more arm strength than he had as a rookie. And he displayed an adept touch on the deep ball, something that certainly caught the eye of his teammates and coaches.

"You've always got to want to play and improve," Rodgers said. "I think if you're content with being a backup, you're not going to last long in this league, although obviously I know my role on this team.

"I'm the backup to one of the greatest quarterbacks of all time, and I know that until he's ready to call it quits, be it end of this year, end of next year, end of the

Jim Biever

year after that, I know my role. But at the same time, the attitude I have to have is one of mainly working on things to get better and always looking for ways to improve."

Unfortunately for Rodgers, once the season started, he had to look awfully hard for ways to keep getting better. Favre had a bounce-back year in 2006, and Rodgers saw precious little time on Sundays.

To Rodgers' credit, though, his day-to-day consistency was a real strength. Rodgers made the most of his limited repetitions in practice, he continued to master the offense through film study, and he became a popular figure in the Packers' locker room.

"He practices like he's ready," Green Bay tight end Bubba Franks said. "You never know until you put him in, but he's practicing like he's the starter, which has got to give him a little confidence. The coach lets him go with the (No.) 1s, and he gets good reps. But right now, no one's sure how he'll do until he gets out there and does it."

Rodgers saw action in just two games that season and struggled. He finished with a 48.2 passer rating

In Aaron Rodgers' first season in Green Bay, he played in just three games and had a paltry passer rating of 39.8.

"I'M THE BACKUP TO ONE OF THE GREATEST QUARTERBACKS OF ALL TIME AND I KNOW THAT UNTIL HE'S READY TO CALL IT QUITS, BE IT END OF THIS YEAR, END OF NEXT YEAR, END OF THE YEAR AFTER THAT, I KNOW MY ROLE."

—Aaron Rodgers

after completing just six of 15 passes for 46 yards and didn't have an interception or touchdown pass. The most frustrating afternoon of Rodgers' season came during a 35–0 home loss to mighty New England in late November. Favre left the game late in the first half with an elbow injury and the Packers trailing 21–0.

Rodgers had a chance to show the fan base what the future might look like. Instead, they had to be longing for the past after Rodgers went just 4-of-12 for 32 yards, took three sacks, and fumbled once.

"I think I put him in a tough situation trying to get out there and throw the ball every time," McCarthy said. "I thought sometimes he got out of the offense, but I thought he made some plays with his feet. I think you see his athletic ability. It was a great test for his preparation, how important it is for the backup quarterback to prepare harder and more than the starter.... He was put in a tough spot."

Adding injury to insult, Rodgers suffered a broken foot and spent the final six weeks of the regular season on injured reserve.

"He's got talent, he has ability, he has know-how," McCarthy insisted of Rodgers. "When his opportunity comes, I want to put my foot on the gas and go with him. The only thing you don't know with a quarterback until he gets a chance is if he can lead your offense."

Still, as Rodgers' second season in Green Bay came to a close, the jury was still out. Rodgers had improved immensely during an impressive summer. But that didn't carry over to his brief playing opportunities in the regular season. And now, two years into his young career, Rodgers' passer rating was a paltry 43.9.

"All I can do is keep working hard," Rodgers said. "I think guys respect someone that comes to work every day and puts his heart and soul into this, and I think I do. And even though I'm not playing, I think guys see my enthusiasm, the way I care about the guys and cheerlead for other guys, and they respect that. And when my time comes, I'll be ready."

Per usual, the Packers had no idea when that time would be.

Green Bay closed the regular season with a bang, winning its final four games and improving to 8–8. After the season finale in Chicago that year, Favre cried on national television, giving many the impression he'd retire. So as the Packers exited Green Bay that January, they had no idea if the Rodgers' era would start in 2007. Just in case, Green Bay's brass was putting on a brave face.

"I think Aaron Rodgers is a young man that has excellent ability," McCarthy said. "Mentally he has an excellent understanding and the ability to comprehend and communicate our system. I think he's done a very good job in the time we've been together in preparing himself, going through quarterback school last year. We'll take the same path this year, so I look for him to improve."

Just how much—and how soon—depended largely on Favre.

• •

Legendary UCLA basketball coach John Wooden had several axioms for life. Among them were the following:

• Flexibility is the key to stability.
• Failure to prepare is preparing to fail.
• Be quick, but don't hurry.

All would have been applicable to Rodgers in the 2007 season.

By Year 3 of his apprenticeship under Favre, Rodgers felt like he was ready to lead Green Bay. But after the Packers closed the 2006 season with four straight wins, Favre took just four weeks—a relatively short amount of time for him—to declare he'd be back for a 16th season in Green Bay. The previous offseason, Favre had waited until April to announce he'd be back.

"I am so excited about coming back," Favre said. "We have a good nucleus of young players. We were 8–8 last year, and that's encouraging. My offensive line looks good, the defense played good down the stretch. I'm excited about playing for a talented young football team."

Publicly, Rodgers said all the right things. But deep down, Rodgers believed he was ready to take over. He proved it again that summer by lighting it up during training camp. Rodgers had several chances to play with the No. 1 offense during preseason games that summer, and for the most part, he shined.

In Green Bay's second preseason game against Seattle, Rodgers was 5-of-7 for 58 yards, one TD, and a 135.7 quarterback rating while working with the first-team offense. One week later against Jacksonville, Rodgers was 5-of-7 for 71 yards, zero TDs, and a 103.9 rating when leading the No. 1s.

"I'm not trying to be glib, but I've liked him all along," Packers general manager Ted Thompson said of Rodgers. "Yeah, he went through some tough times, but preseason games and that sort of thing, and even the game he played in last year, I don't think necessarily is the telling tale. I think he's a young man that's confident, that's smart, that is physically talented, that believes he can play, and he has understood and accepted the role that he's in, even though he still wants to play. I'm proud of the way he carries himself. I think he's going to be a good player, and I'm pleased with the way he's playing now."

By the time summer ended, it was apparent Green Bay had an extremely gifted second-string quarterback.

Chico Enterprise-Record/Jason Halley

Aaron Rodgers chats with (left to right) his agent Michael Sullivan, his father, Ed, his brothers, Luke and Jordan, and his mother, Darla, after the Packers beat the 49ers 30–19 in San Francisco on December 10, 2006.

The uncertain, hesitant, indecisive player of 2005 was gone. Now, Rodgers was playing fast, confident, and with total certainty.

"Confidence wise, it probably hasn't wavered that much," Rodgers said. "But comfort wise, I think that's the most important thing. Now for me, I'm confident and comfortable within the offense, and I just feel like the game is able to slow down for me. I'm able to go through my progressions...and for me it's just getting to a comfort level. And I feel like I'm getting closer to that."

Rodgers finished that summer with a passer rating of 98.3, threw three TDs, and had no interceptions. But when the season began, it was back to watching and waiting. And what Rodgers watched was a brilliant season by Favre and the Packers. Green Bay began the year 10–1, and Favre was playing at an MVP level.

"All I can do is keep practicing hard, keep studying, and if I do get the chance to play, just go out there and make the most of it," Rodgers said that November.

Shockingly, that chance came in Green Bay's biggest regular season game in a decade. Surprisingly, Rodgers was the star. Green Bay went to Dallas for a battle of 10–1 teams, where the winner had the inside track to homefield advantage throughout the NFC playoffs. Favre played miserably, threw two early interceptions, then exited with an elbow injury and with the Packers in a 27–10 hole.

With 9 minutes, 53 seconds left in the second quarter, Rodgers entered the huddle of what had been a lifeless offense. The Packers were down three scores, and little had gone right. Over the next two-plus hours, Rodgers showed Packer Nation there would indeed be life after Favre.

On the Packers' second possession with Rodgers in charge, he engineered an 8-play, 74-yard touchdown drive that pulled Green Bay to within 27–17 at halftime. Wideout Greg Jennings made the play of the drive by taking a short out route and turning it into a 43-yard gain. Rodgers and Jennings then hooked up for an 11-yard TD just 31 seconds before halftime.

On Green Bay's first drive of the second half, Rodgers was back at it again. This time, he led a 12-play, 69-yard march that pulled the Packers to within 27–24.

"To me, Aaron Rodgers played way better than Brett Favre," Cowboys linebacker Bradie James said afterward. "Brett Favre was just throwing the ball up. I don't know if we'd rather have him in there or Rodgers."

Green Bay never could get over the hump and fell, 37–27, in a game that eventually gave the Cowboys the NFC's top seed. But Rodgers won a lot of people over with his performance that night. He finished the game 18-of-26 for 201 yards, his first NFL touchdown, and an impressive quarterback rating of 104.8.

"I just can't say enough about his preparation, because I didn't even blink," Packers coach Mike McCarthy said of Rodgers. "I didn't throw anything out. I've been in that position before when you have to go to your backup or go to your third guy or even your fourth guy. I went through it in San Francisco, and you

(opposite) Aaron Rodgers rolls out to pass during a 2006 preseason game against the Titans. Rodgers rarely left the sideline during the 2006 regular season. He played in just two games and had a 48.2 passer rating. (above) By 2007, Aaron Rodgers was playing like a No. 1 draft pick...but Brett Favre's high level of play left Rodgers wearing a headset for most of the season.

just start crossing plays off the chart, and that wasn't the case. I thought Aaron did an excellent job."

Even Favre—who was far from the ideal mentor—sang Rodgers' praises afterward.

"I thought he played great," Favre said of Rodgers. "He gave us a chance to win. I thought he was ready to play. I was hoping it would be in different circumstances...but I thought he did a fine job."

While Rodgers answered many questions that night, more were soon to arise. The week after the Dallas game, Rodgers suffered a hamstring injury in practice and was inactive the final four weeks of the regular season. That marked the second straight season Rodgers missed substantial time, and many wondered if he could stay on the field.

Of course, the way Favre was going that season, it didn't matter much. Favre finished that regular season

(top) Aaron Rodgers and Brett Favre looked loose during this 2007 practice, but neither knew that they faced a tense transition in the months ahead. (bottom) Rodgers impressed a national television audience with a gutsy November 2007 performance against the Cowboys in relief of an injured Favre. Green Bay may have lost the game but the team discovered its future starter.

> # "I THINK HE'S A YOUNG MAN THAT'S CONFIDENT, THAT'S SMART, THAT IS PHYSICALLY TALENTED, THAT BELIEVES HE CAN PLAY, AND HE HAS UNDERSTOOD AND ACCEPTED THE ROLE THAT HE'S IN, EVEN THOUGH HE STILL WANTS TO PLAY. I'M PROUD OF THE WAY HE CARRIES HIMSELF."
>
> **—Ted Thompson**

with 28 touchdowns, 15 interceptions, and a passer rating of 95.7. Green Bay went 13–3, earned the No. 2 seed in the postseason, and Favre finished second in the MVP voting to New England's Tom Brady.

"I just think he's doing a great job of running the offense," McCarthy said of Favre late that season. "We've asked him to do some things. We've asked him to do more of things that he hasn't had to do a lot of in the past. I'm talking more spread offense and taking advantage of [things] at the line-of-scrimmage situations. So he's done a very good job."

The Packers defeated Seattle in the NFC Divisional Game, 42–20. But their year ended in heartbreak with a 23–20 overtime loss to the visiting New York Giants in the NFC Championship Game. Favre struggled that night, and his overtime interception led to a game-winning field goal by the Giants' Lawrence Tynes. Still, as the Packers left that offseason, no one expected the 38-year-old Favre to call it quits. He was still playing at an elite level, the Packers were one game from the Super Bowl, and their future was remarkably bright.

"I said, 'You going to give me one more year?' He just kind of giggled," wideout Greg Jennings said. "I did the same thing last year, and he said, 'We'll see,' and he was back. Who knows? Hopefully he's back.

We'd definitely like to see him in that locker over there one more time."

Rodgers himself expected Favre back. And when Rodgers left Lambeau Field that frigid January night, he still had no idea what his own future in Green Bay held.

Little did Rodgers know that the months ahead were soon to be filled with drama, drama, and more drama. ∎

Aaron Rodgers and Brett Favre became closer during the 2007 season, but that was all about to change during the crazy summer of 2008.

A MESSY TRANSITION

It was March 4, 2008, and Aaron Rodgers' life had just gotten a whole lot crazier. By 7:00 AM that day, Rodgers had received eight phone calls and a bevy of text messages. Could it be? Apparently it could. Brett Favre was set to call it quits. The Green Bay Packers were now officially Rodgers' team.

"I'm in a good situation, I've got a great team around me," Rodgers said shortly after news of Favre's retirement broke. "A lot of people have been focusing on what I'm going to do. It's what the team is going to do, really. I'm an important part of that, and I know my role. I need to play well, and I'm not really going to have a grace period either. The expectations that people are going to have are very high. The expectations I have of myself are very high as well. I've definitely been told there haven't been a lot of guys following a legend that play well. Hopefully I'll have like a Steve Young kind of experience here."

Rodgers, a passionate San Francisco 49ers fan as a child, watched closely when Young replaced the legendary Joe Montana in 1992. Although Young eventually guided the 49ers to a championship in Super Bowl XXIX, not all San Francisco fans were rejoicing.

"I know a lot of friends and family who were Joe Montana fans who it didn't matter how good Steve Young did," Rodgers said. "They weren't going to cheer for him because he wasn't Joe Montana."

In many ways, Rodgers could relate. Rodgers' three-year waiting period had at times felt like 30. Those three seasons, though, had given Rodgers an opportunity to learn the intricacies of Green Bay's offense, study defenses, and pick up some tricks from Favre. Much of Packer Nation, though, was devastated by the news of Favre's departure. Green Bay's iconic quarterback had been brilliant in 2007 and most expected Favre back in 2008.

To those fans looking for the nearest bridge, Rodgers had the following message.

"I'm not Brett Favre," Rodgers said. "If [fans] want me to be the next Brett Favre, I'm not going to be him. I'm Aaron Rodgers. That's who I am. I'm going to be the best quarterback I can be. He did it his way, and I'm going to do it my way, and hopefully I can be successful."

Despite Rodgers' minimal game experience, the Packers were remarkably confident moving forward with him. In fact, at the 2008 NFL Combine, one Packers assistant coach said he believed Green Bay would have won the Super Bowl in '07 if Rodgers had been the starter. No one will ever know that answer, but Rodgers had become far more comfortable with the NFL game since arriving, something he showed during that stellar performance in Dallas in 2007. Rodgers had also formed a tight bond with several teammates,

Green Bay Packers quarterback Brett Favre gets choked up when announcing his retirement on March 6, 2008.

"IF (FANS) WANT ME TO BE THE NEXT BRETT FAVRE, I'M NOT GOING TO BE HIM. I'M AARON RODGERS. THAT'S WHO I AM. I'M GOING TO BE THE BEST QUARTERBACK I CAN BE. HE DID IT HIS WAY, AND I'M GOING TO DO IT MY WAY."

—Aaron Rodgers

earned the respect of the locker room, and tried becoming a leader.

"I like the fact that he has come into a situation that is difficult, and he has taken on those responsibilities," Packers general manager Ted Thompson said. "The fans haven't seen him, but he goes out to practice every day, he's very well received by his teammates, he and Brett got along well, he understood his role. That's a difficult thing to do for a young man that wants to play. So, I think he's positioned himself as a leader even though he wasn't playing, and I think he's positioned himself to be a leader going forward."

Packers coach Mike McCarthy echoed Thompson's sentiments. "I have zero concerns about Aaron Rodgers," McCarthy said. "I think his time is now. He's ready to go, and he will have another offseason to prepare for that. We need to make sure that we're ready for the whole quarterback position, and that is our focus."

Rodgers had been preparing throughout the off-season as though he'd be Favre's backup for a fourth straight year. But in the blink of an eye, Rodgers went from obscurity to the spotlight.

"I'm always going to be compared to Brett, obviously," Rodgers said. "I think I just need to be my own quarterback, be my own man.

"And I think the most important thing...to me was the texts I got from my teammates—just the encouragement. I've always felt like they believe in me just because they see my work ethic. But just to have that reinforced by some of the text messages and calls I got was pretty special."

In the months ahead, Rodgers probably thought back to many of those messages. Because things inside Green Bay's organization were about to get a whole lot messier.

....

April and May came with barely a whimper in tiny Green Bay. On April 25, the Packers placed Favre on the reserve-retired list and announced plans to retire his No. 4 jersey in the regular-season opener against Minnesota. During April's NFL Draft, the Packers used a second-round pick on quarterback Brian Brohm of Louisville. The Packers later used a seventh rounder on quarterback Matt Flynn of LSU.

Those picks were made largely for depth, though, as the Packers didn't have another quarterback on the roster.

"Mike said I'm the guy. Ted said I'm the guy," Rodgers said when asked if he might have to battle Brohm for the starting job. "Brian looks like he's a good player. He's smart, he's picking up the offense pretty well. But it's really in my hands. If I play well, everything's going to take care of itself. And if I don't, either Brian or somebody else will be replacing me, and I'll know before anybody else."

Of that trio, Rodgers truly had little to worry about. Brohm was overmatched from the start and lasted just one season in Green Bay. Flynn performed far better than a typical seventh-round draft choice, but he was light years behind Rodgers.

Clearly, this was Rodgers' team now. And when Green Bay gathered for its first organized team activity session in May, Rodgers was the clear-cut starter and was downright giddy about the opportunity that awaited.

"It feels great," Rodgers said. "I've taken the No. 1 reps in practice throughout the last three years, but to know that I'm the guy going into the season is pretty exciting, because guys are starting to rally around my leadership style and the way I do things. Like I said, I've been waiting for this experience, this opportunity, my whole life, so it's pretty exciting."

Many of Rodgers' teammates shared that excitement.

"It's becoming a catch phrase, but we're all excited," left guard Daryn Colledge said. "Everyone misses Brett. Everyone loves Brett and his humor and all that. But we're such a young team that I think there's just a ton of excitement out there right now. There's kind of a buzz right now, and we want to prove everybody wrong.

"We don't want to be that team that was 13–3 and then doesn't make the playoffs. We want to build a dynasty. We want to do it with Aaron. I think he's going to bring a whole different dynamic than Brett. He's the kind of guy that most guys will definitely go to battle for."

That spring, Rodgers was a different quarterback from the one who arrived in Green Bay three years earlier. He had lowered his body fat and was in the best physical shape of his life. Rodgers no longer held the ball near his ear like he did back in 2005. And McCarthy had worked extensively on Rodgers' footwork with terrific results.

"I think he's gotten better, no question," Packers offensive coordinator Joe Philbin said. "He was a young guy still...and there's no question he's improved. He moves well and fluidly. He's a fluid athlete. He's throwing some competitive balls down the field."

He sure was. That entire spring, Rodgers was throwing the ball with more power and accuracy than any time since his arrival in Green Bay. Rodgers' arm strength had been questioned before the NFL Draft in 2005, which is one reason he slid to No. 24 that year. But watching Rodgers hum balls around the Don Hutson Center that May and June, you had to wonder how so many NFL scouts could be wrong.

"He could always throw the ball. I was at his college workout, and his arm strength was never a factor in my opinion," said McCarthy, who was one of the people who passed on Rodgers during that 2005 draft. "But I definitely do think he throws it probably better now than he did; just overall his body, his conditioning, and his strength have improved. I would say he does throw maybe with more velocity than he initially did. Aaron Rodgers has a strong arm, always has in my experience with him."

Still, most national "experts" were predicting failure for Rodgers. Of course, all they had to judge Rodgers on was seven career games, in which his passer rating was 73.3. But Rodgers was doing all he could to ignore the critics.

"I try not to [pay attention]," Rodgers said. "I watch Lost and The Office when I watch TV. But I have a lot of friends, and that stuff means a lot to them so I hear just about everything that anybody says.

"My family and I, we've had conversations about not worrying about what other people say about me. Because the only people whose opinions I really care about, no disrespect to anybody in the media, are the 53 guys in the locker room, our personnel department, our coaching staff."

By the end of mini-camps that June, the Packers were confident in what they had. Rodgers had done all they'd hoped, and Green Bay's coaching staff felt extremely certain they could build on their 2007 successes.

"I've been setting myself up mentally for this for a while," Rodgers said. "It's exciting, it really is, to know that I'm going to get first shot, that I'm the guy, and really my own destiny is in my hands. If I play well, everything is going to take care of itself."

Or would it? On June 20—the final day of offseason practices—McCarthy took a call from Favre, who told his coach he still had an "itch" to play and wanted back in.

"When he picked up the phone again after he dropped it, he said, 'Oh, God, Brett. You're putting us in a tight spot,'" Favre later said of his conversation with McCarthy. "He said, 'Brett, playing here is not an option.' Those were his exact, exact words."

What had been a quiet three months in Green Bay had just gotten a whole lot louder. And things were only getting started.

. . . .

Green Bay's players soon went off for some R&R before training camp. Favre and the Packers, though, turned their saga into a nightly soap opera. Favre continued to tell the Packers he wanted to come back. Green Bay's decision makers continued to tell him no. Both sides made their stances very public, and Rodgers had no choice but to watch it all play out.

"I realized back in 2005 that the only things I need to worry about are the things I can control," Rodgers said. "And I can't control the decision that the organization makes, or Brett's decisions. So I can control my preparation and my effort and my focus, and that's what I'm trying to do."

Still, the constant back and forth was brutal for all parties.

On July 8, Favre met with McCarthy and Thompson and told them both he still wanted to play. The Packers' brass tried talking Favre out of that decision. On July 11, Favre asked the Packers for his release so he could return to the NFL with another team. Green Bay, believing that Favre wanted to return to the NFC North with either Minnesota or Chicago, denied his request.

"The finality of his decision to retire was accepted by the organization," the Packers said in a team statement. "At that point, the Green Bay Packers made the commitment to move forward with our football team."

On July 17, the Packers accused the Vikings of tampering, something that was never proven. Favre did not show up for the start of training camp on July 27, but two days later he faxed his official request for reinstatement to the NFL.

Day after day, Rodgers was bombarded by a bevy of questions—and very few were about anything happening on the field.

"I don't need people to feel sorry for me," Rodgers said. "Playing quarterback is a tough job, and there's a lot of scrutiny that goes along with that. You get too much blame a lot of times; you get too much credit a lot of times. And you just have to stay balanced and stay even-keeled. The last three years and this offseason have made me the person I am today, and I wouldn't have changed it for anything."

On July 30, Packers president Mark Murphy flew to Mississippi and offered Favre a lucrative marketing deal to stay retired: 10 years, $20 million. Favre rejected the offer and flew to Green Bay on July 31. Two nights later, during the Packers' annual "Family Night" scrimmage at Lambeau Field, Rodgers heard a mixture of boos and cheers when he was introduced.

"Yeah, I take it personally," Rodgers said. "But like I said, it's not the first time, and it won't be the last time."

With Favre's shadow looming large, Rodgers struggled that night, missing six straight passes at one point and throwing an interception to safety Aaron Rouse.

One day later, NFL Commissioner Roger Goodell reinstated Favre, and it appeared the Packers would hold an open competition for the quarterback job.

"I'm a competitor. I'm going to compete," Rodgers said. "This isn't going to be easy. It's going to be a dogfight. And I know if they do open it up to competition, not a lot of people give me a chance, but I believe in myself, and I'm going to be the best I can be and let coach decide from there."

McCarthy insisted that he still hadn't made up his mind about how to proceed.

"There have been no promises," McCarthy said. "Once again, there has been indecision throughout Brett's path back here to Green Bay. It's important for us to sit down and communicate."

Over the next two days, Favre and McCarthy met for nearly six hours in what McCarthy termed "brutally honest conversations." When it was over, the two sides agreed that it was best if Favre didn't remain with the Packers.

"The train has left the station, whatever analogy you want," McCarthy said. "He needs to jump on the train, and let's go. Or, if we can't get past things that have happened, I have to keep the train moving."

So on August 5, Favre flew home to Mississippi, and the next day he was traded to the New York Jets for a third-round draft choice.

"This is, in many ways, sad that this is where it came to," Thompson said. "At the end of the day though, I think all parties involved felt like it was the best solution to a very difficult situation."

Finally, once and for all, the Packers were Rodgers' team. He had played the role of good soldier well through all the chaos, saying all the right things and never losing faith that he would keep the starting job the organization handed him months earlier.

"It was a difficult situation," Rodgers said. "It was tough to stand up every day in front of the media not knowing what questions were coming at me and how the fans were going to react that day in practice. But the whole time the organization stood by me, and they told the truth, and I told the truth, and we moved on together.

"I think they knew what kind of person they were getting, and at the same time I hope they knew what kind of player they were getting as well. It gave me a lot of confidence that they stood by me through everything that happened. It was a trying time for myself and the organization, but the fact that they continued to stand by me and believe in me was definitely big for my confidence."

Rodgers had won half the battle: keeping his job. Now came the harder part: winning football games. ■

Two days after Brett Favre's retirement press conference, Aaron Rodgers spoke confidently about leading the Packers into the future.

A NEW STARTER IN GREEN BAY

The rest of that crazy summer of 2008 went without incident. The Packers were 1–3 that preseason, but Rodgers played at a high level throughout. He finished with a 103.6 passer rating and had the backing of his teammates.

"Nothing changes," wideout Donald Driver said. "We don't do anything different than we've been doing when Brett was here. The play calling is going to stay the same. Cadence is going to stay the same. Nothing different. You just see a different face, and we all move on. And I think that's the big thing with us."

Still, the Favre-a-palooza had dragged on for more than a month and turned much of Green Bay's preseason into a circus. Needless to say, the Packers were excited for the regular season to begin.

"Can't wait," wideout Greg Jennings said. "It's really been a long summer. Can't wait to get going."

Neither could Rodgers, who anxiously awaited his first NFL start. Fittingly, it came against NFC North rival Minnesota, a team that had geared its offseason around catching Green Bay. And the entire football world would be watching, as Packers-Vikings was being shown on Monday Night Football.

Roughly an hour before kickoff, Rodgers plopped down next to wideout Ruvell Martin inside the Green Bay Packers locker room. Rodgers was about to become the first quarterback not named Brett Favre to start a game for Green Bay in nearly 16 years. He was set to replace a living legend and the finest player in franchise history. And he was trying to win over a fan base that was still largely bitter over Favre's departure.

So clearly, Rodgers was bouncing off the walls, right?

"No," said Martin, who was Rodgers' best friend on the team. "He was calm as can be."

Which is how Rodgers proceeded to play.

Rodgers certainly didn't make anyone forget Favre during his first NFL start. But he was efficient, accurate, and managed the game extremely well as the Packers notched a huge 24–19 win at Lambeau Field. Rodgers finished the night 18-of-22 for 178 yards, threw for a touchdown, ran for another, and posted a passer rating of 115.5. He also rushed for 35 yards and wasn't sacked a single time.

"It feels great," Rodgers said on a night when he was among the last to leave the Packers' locker room. "You've got to remind yourself it's just one win, but it was a big one. I think the talk this week was a lot about the Vikings and I don't think enough about the kind of team that we had. So we definitely wanted to play well tonight, and I think we did."

With all eyes focused on Rodgers, he certainly did his part. All Rodgers had to do in his first start was fill the shoes of the NFL's all-time leader in passing yards, touchdowns, and wins. Making things even more uncomfortable for Rodgers was the fact that Favre had

Aaron Rodgers was outstanding in the 2008 preseason, then led the Packers past the Minnesota Vikings in his first-ever career start.

"HE PLAYED GREAT, MADE GOOD DECISIONS, AND I THINK HE WON THE RESPECT OF A LOT OF PEOPLE. I THINK A LOT OF PEOPLE HAVE MORE FAITH IN HIM NOW. —Korey Hall

excelled in his New York Jets debut with a passer rating of 125.9.

But Rodgers never blinked. For the most part, he kept his passes short and simple. The Packers used more max protection than in 2007, largely to slow Minnesota's vaunted pass rush. And Rodgers took very few chances in the passing game. Still, he did enough to lift his team to a huge win.

"He did what he had to do," Vikings cornerback Cedric Griffin said of Rodgers. "Nothing special. Nothing great. But he executed real well, and they won the game. Congratulations to him."

Minnesota linebacker Chad Greenway agreed.

"I'd say he did his thing," Greenway said. "He didn't kill us, but he kept the chains moving and kind of picked away at us. He was efficient."

That he was.

Green Bay's offense was brutal early on, some of it the fault of Rodgers, but much the responsibility of a reworked offensive line. The Packers had five first quarter penalties—all on the offensive line—and managed just 43 yards of total offense. Rodgers and Green Bay's attack finally got going in the second quarter, though, when they went to work on Minnesota's suspect passing defense.

On the Packers' first play of the second quarter, Rodgers unleashed a bomb for Jennings. Green Bay's top wideout adjusted nicely and made a 56-yard reception in front of Minnesota reserve corner Charles Gordon at the Minnesota 6-yard line. That set up a 1-yard TD pass from Rodgers to fullback Korey Hall on third-and-goal that gave the Packers a 7–3 lead.

"You know, I don't think he could have handled this whole situation better," Hall later said of Rodgers. "You can't imagine the amount of pressure he has on his shoulders right now, and he went out and was collected and calm. He played great, made good decisions, and I think he won the respect of a lot of people. I think a lot of people have more faith in him now. I think he's going to have a great season."

Later in the second quarter, Rodgers engineered an 8-play, 63-yard march that set up a 42-yard Mason Crosby field goal and gave Green Bay a 10–3 advantage. At halftime, Rodgers had completed 75 percent of his 16 attempts for 139 yards, with a passer rating of 121.6.

Rodgers wasn't asked to do much in the second half, thanks to a 76-yard punt return for a TD by Will Blackmon and a 57-yard run by Ryan Grant to the Vikings' 2-yard line. Grant's burst set Rodgers up for a 1-yard TD that made it 24–12 and provided what proved to be the game-winning points.

"I thought Aaron Rodgers played well," Packers coach Mike McCarthy said afterward. "Number one, I thought he managed the game...I thought he did a good job managing the game without taking chances. Playing with the play call and taking what the defense gave you and so forth. So I was pleased with his performance tonight."

Afterward, Rodgers knew this was nothing more than a single start. There were still 15 games remaining, and no one was mentioning Rodgers in the same breath with Favre. But Rodgers' first impression certainly was a favorable one.

Aaron Rodgers (left) celebrates with injured teammate Ruvell Martin after throwing a touchdown pass against the Detroit Lions in Week 2, 2008.

"It was good to get the first one under your belt and move forward now," he said. "It was a huge game for us. That's what it was made out to be, and I feel like it was....And although we didn't play as well as we wanted to on offense, I felt like we beat a very good football team, and we're excited about being 1–0."

Rodgers also played well the next week at Detroit, helping the Packers rally for a 48–25 win. Green Bay trailed, 25–24, midway through the fourth quarter before scoring the final 24 points of the game. Rodgers was sharp again, completing 24-of-38 for 328 yards and three TDs. Rodgers' first road start also produced his first fourth-quarter comeback, and he became the first Green Bay quarterback to start his career 2–0 since Scott Hunter in 1971.

"I thought Aaron put together a fine performance," McCarthy said. "There are a couple of things he can learn from. I thought he did a really good job of using his feet to stay out of bad situations; very decisive with the ball. I thought he threw the ball very well today. I thought he had a real nice day today."

Rodgers threw all three of his TD passes in the first 24 minutes of the game as the Packers raced to a 21–0 lead. Then, after the Lions had rallied back to take a one-point lead, Rodgers hit Jennings with a 60-yard pass to set up the go-ahead field goal. Green Bay never trailed again.

"My idol growing up, Joe Montana, was a guy who could always bring his team back in the fourth quarter, a guy who his teammates trusted with the ball in his hands late in the game," Rodgers said. "You don't want to have a lot of comebacks because you want to be ahead in the game, but unfortunately our lead dwindled. Detroit got the crowd back in the game, and we were able to put together really one big play, Greg Jennings with a big catch and run, and then a big field goal by Mason (Crosby)."

The Packers were 2-0, sitting atop the NFC North, and looking pretty good for staying with Rodgers instead Favre. Over the next few weeks, that would all change. Green Bay's slide started with a 27–16 home loss to Dallas. Ironically, Rodgers' play against those same Cowboys 10 months earlier was a big reason the Packers' brass felt confident cutting the cord with Favre.

Rodgers didn't do anything to submarine Green Bay's chances of defeating the Cowboys. But he wasn't special, either. Rodgers finished the night 22-of-39 for 290 yards with no touchdowns and no interceptions. However, 146 of Rodgers' passing yards came in the fourth quarter when the contest had been decided.

"You've got to give Dallas credit," Rodgers said afterward. "I didn't have a lot of lanes tonight, didn't throw the ball as well as I wanted to, and they did a nice job with their pass rush."

For Rodgers, it was a major difference from the first two weeks of the year in which he'd made Packer Nation stop clamoring for Favre—at least temporarily.

In Green Bay's wins over Minnesota and Detroit, Rodgers had posted a lights-out passer rating of 117.8. He had completed 70.0 percent of his throws with four touchdowns and no interceptions. Rodgers never could get the offense on track against Dallas, though. Rodgers was too slow with his progressions and took five sacks, the most a Green Bay quarterback had taken since Sept. 17, 2000. The Packers were just 1-for-3 in the red zone and converted only 4-of-14 third downs (28.6 percent).

"We wanted to get him uncomfortable and make him run around a little bit," Dallas defensive end Marcus Spears said. "He was able to scramble against other teams, so our rush lanes were very important. We also wanted to get our hands up and cover receivers downfield. Overall, we did a pretty good job."

Unfortunately for Rodgers and the Packers, this was just the start of an ugly skid. The next week, Rodgers threw three interceptions, had a passer rating of just 55.9, and the Packers fell in Tampa Bay, 30–21. Of greater concern, though, was the fact that Rodgers suffered a sprained throwing shoulder and couldn't finish the game.

Throughout the following week, Rodgers' status for Green Bay's Week 5 home game with Atlanta was up in the air.

"My understanding is the strength is definitely improving, and I'm sure there's going to be some pain as he works through the progress of the evaluation," McCarthy said two days before the Falcons' game. "Frankly, you hand in the inactives at 10:30 [AM], and I'm sure we'll make our decision close to then."

By that time, Rodgers had shown enough improvement to start against the Falcons. Rodgers had a big day, too, throwing for 313 yards, three TDs, and posting a 109.4 passer rating. But with the Packers trailing, 20–17 midway through the fourth quarter and trying to rally, Rodgers was intercepted by Atlanta's Michael Boley. The Falcons scored three plays later and held on for a 27–24 win.

Green Bay had fallen to 2–3, the same number of losses it suffered in all of 2007. The Packers' losing streak was now three games, and the toughest part of their schedule was looming.

"You don't push the panic button," Packers cornerback Tramon Williams said. "All you can do is go back to the drawing board and clean up mistakes you've

Packers head coach Mike McCarthy, part of the San Francisco 49ers staff that passed on drafting Aaron Rodgers, was thrilled to have him in Green Bay.

been making. The problem is they aren't new mistakes. They're the same mistakes we've been making all year long, and we still haven't fixed them. I guess that's troubling."

Green Bay solved some of those problems the following week with a 27–17 win at Seattle. Rodgers then notched his biggest NFL win, a 34–14 victory over Peyton Manning and Indianapolis.

"Peyton's a great quarterback," Rodgers said. "He's established. He's been to a number of Pro Bowls. He's won a Super Bowl, he's won MVPs. I hope one day to be able to be mentioned in the same sentence more than just when we play them. But I haven't proven anything that he's proven yet."

On this night, though, Rodgers got the better of Manning. Rodgers was an extremely steady 21-of-28 for 186 yards and one TD pass. Manning, on the other hand, completed just 21-of-42 passes and was intercepted twice.

Now, heading into the bye week, the Packers had new life. Green Bay was 4–3, had a two-game winning streak, and was tied atop the NFC North with Chicago.

"I think it's just a big confidence boost for our team," Rodgers said. "We were 3–3 coming into this one and...felt like we needed this going into the bye week."

The bye week turned out to be an eventful period for Rodgers. During that two-week stretch, negotiations heated up for a contract extension, and Rodgers eventually signed a six-year, $66 million extension.

"As we talked about in the past, we try to be proactive in our discussions with our current players, and we felt like this was an appropriate time to try to come to an agreement with Aaron," Packers general manager Ted Thompson said. "We feel like this is good for the organization and the players, and we will continue this approach as we move forward."

At the time, Rodgers had made just seven career starts. But the Packers believed in what they saw, and Rodgers believed in the Packers.

"It means a lot," Rodgers said of signing the long-term deal. "I'm very excited knowing that my future is going to be here in Green Bay."

The immediate future, though, became an exercise in frustration. First, the Packers fell in overtime to undefeated Tennessee, 19–16. Then Green Bay dropped a 28–27 decision at Minnesota when Mason Crosby narrowly missed a 52-yard field goal in the closing seconds.

Those losses left the Packers 0–3 in games decided by four points or fewer. And at 4–5, Green Bay's season was hanging by a thread.

"The critical situations that we haven't been able to overcome, it's the National Football League," McCarthy said. "You can break it down to explosive gains, negative plays, the different things that go on, and the factor hasn't fallen on our side. We have to continue to work, continue to make those critical plays at critical times, and we haven't done that. We have five losses, and you can point to specific plays in every single one of those games. We need to turn some of those around in our favor."

The Packers showed signs of life the following week with a 37–3 dismantling of Chicago. Rodgers led the charge, completing 23-of-30 passes for 227 yards and two TDs. Now, with six games remaining, the Packers, Bears, and Vikings were all tied for the division lead with 5–5 records.

"It's going to be very exciting for all of us," Rodgers said after the game. "We feel like we're going to have to win every game. We control our own destiny now because I know we have the tie-breaker over Chicago, and we have the division tie-breaker over Minnesota. So we couldn't ask for a better position. It's been an up-and-down season, but we played the way we feel we're capable of playing [against Chicago], and we're very confident."

That confidence was shattered, though, over the next month. Remarkably, Green Bay lost five straight games—its longest slide since 1990—and completely fell out of the playoff picture.

Aaron Rodgers' ability to escape the pocket and beat defenses with his legs was a dimension of the quarterback position the Packers hadn't enjoyed for years.

"TO BE HONEST...I'M GETTING KIND OF TIRED OF LEARNING FROM EXPERIENCES LIKE THIS.

—Aaron Rodgers

The Packers were routed by New Orleans, 51–29, on a Monday night. But Green Bay's next four losses were by a combined 14 points, and it had chances to win each game. In a 35–31 home loss to Carolina, Rodgers was white hot much of the day, throwing for 298 yards and three TDs. But with a chance to rally his team late, Rodgers badly underthrew Donald Driver, and Panthers middle linebacker Jon Beason intercepted.

"To be honest with you, I'm getting kind of tired of learning from experiences like this," said Rodgers, whose team fell to 5–7 after the loss. "It's pretty frustrating when you lose games like that. You've got to be critical of yourself. I feel like I competed today, but I didn't throw the ball as well as I wanted to at times. As a quarterback, you want the ball in your hands under two minutes with a chance to lead your team to victory."

One week later, Texans' kicker Kris Brown drilled a 40-yard field goal on the final play of the game to lift Houston to a 24–21 win at Lambeau Field.

"It's disappointing," Rodgers said. "We had a chance to win. It's kind of gone the same script. We start slow, wait for somebody to make a play. Somebody does, then we start turning it on the offensive side of the ball, get the ball in good position, have an opportunity to win the game, and we don't. So that's probably the most frustrating part."

A 20–16 road loss in Jacksonville came next. The Packers then slid all the way to 5–10 after a 20–17 loss in Chicago. Through it all, Rodgers was putting up big numbers. He just wasn't delivering at crunch time, and the Packers couldn't buy a win if the game was close.

"We've just come up short so many times this year," Rodgers said. "We're not going to make excuses. We've had the opportunity in just about every one of those games. You look at the games we've lost; we've lost with opportunities to win in the last minutes. Make a play and win in the last minutes. We haven't done that."

Green Bay finished the season with a 31–21 win over Detroit, which made the Lions the NFL's first winless team since Tampa Bay in 1976. Rodgers and Driver hooked up on a 71-yard TD to ice the game and ensure the Packers wouldn't fall victim to the hapless Lions.

Still Green Bay's season had been a giant disappointment. In a matter of 11 months, the Packers had gone from playing in an NFC Championship Game to posting a 6–10 record and finishing in third place in a watered-down NFC North.

"We didn't want to lose, no. No we didn't," Rodgers said. "But really it's not on your mind once the game starts. We ourselves, we were on a five-game losing streak, so we needed this one to get some momentum going into the next season."

Afterward, Rodgers was conducting his final press conference of 2008 and had answered 21 questions. That, of course, was nothing compared to the thousands he'd fielded during an exhausting season. As the question-and-answer session was coming to a close, Adam Woullard, a gifted member of the Packers public relations staff, said, "Last one please." Rodgers chimed in, "Make it a good one." Remarkably, no one had anything left. It may have been the first time all season that Rodgers could exhale.

Rodgers' first year as the starter in Green Bay was now behind him, and the Packers' 6–10 record would eat at him throughout the entire offseason. But Rodgers had played well, and Green Bay's future at the position appeared bright. Rodgers threw for 4,038 yards, 28 touchdowns, and just 13 interceptions in that 2008 campaign. He completed 63.6 percent of his passes, and his passer rating was an impressive 93.8.

"I played well in stretches, and I didn't play well at times," Rodgers said. "I think I was a little bit too inconsistent at times, and I'm going to be back to work. I'm going to come back when we start and go through another quarterback school and try to get ready to have an even better year next year."

While the move from Favre to Rodgers was painful, awkward, and extremely drawn out, no one inside Green Bay's organization was looking back.

"I think we definitely made the right move at the quarterback position," McCarthy said of the switch to Rodgers. "I was pleased with the productivity from the quarterback position. From an individual standpoint, I think Aaron Rodgers played at a very steady, steady level, which was a high level based on his statistics. He has given us a baseline, a standard that we will hold him to and the offensive group as we move forward."

Rodgers' success was even more impressive considering he was trying to fill the shoes of arguably the greatest player in Packer history. And with Favre still playing for the New York Jets, his shadow loomed incredibly large all season. But Rodgers handled the circus-like atmosphere throughout training camp with class. Then he played at a relatively high level all season.

"I think the thing that impressed me the most about Aaron was how well he handled himself," Packers No. 2 quarterback Matt Flynn said. "He said all the right things. He did all the right things, and I think he became the leader of this team, for sure."

What Rodgers failed to do was succeed in the clutch. Rodgers had a chance to produce game-winning

drives in the final minutes on eight occasions: Tampa Bay, Atlanta, Tennessee, at Minnesota, Carolina, Houston, Jacksonville, and at Chicago. Rodgers failed all eight times, and in games decided by four points or fewer, the Packers went 0–7.

As Rodgers left Green Bay that December for a trip in Australia, he knew his No. 1 area for growth was late-game situations.

"Yeah, that's the NFL right there," Rodgers said. "Games are won and lost by two or three plays just about every game. We've got to make those plays next year. There's going to be similar situations, we're going to have a lot of our guys back, and we're going to need to win those close games."

Still, the good outweighed the bad with Rodgers. Rodgers' accuracy and arm strength were both better than advertised. His decision-making and command of the offense were impressive. In addition, he fought through a sprained right-shoulder injury and started all 16 games.

That's why the Packers felt awfully good about the quarterbacking situation. "He held true to the type of quarterback that I felt he was going to be as far as his decision-making ability and his ball accuracy," McCarthy said. "That's something that he showed in his opportunities as a young player in our first couple of years here, and he was able to sustain that for 16 games. That's what I was most pleased about.

"There are a number of things he was very positive (in). I thought he was very good outside of the pocket making plays with his feet. I thought he was smart in space. He took a couple of hits earlier in the season that you didn't see later in the season. The beauty of Aaron is he is young, and he has the opportunity to only improve. But I think he has a good baseline to start from."

Indeed he did. And Rodgers was only getting started. ■

2009: MOVING TOWARD THE TOP

As 2009 dawned, there was renewed hope and optimism in the NFL's smallest city. From a team standpoint, the 2008 campaign had been one of the most disappointing in franchise history. In fact, Green Bay's seven-game slide in the standings was the longest single-season skid in team history. Mentally, the year had been even more cumbersome. The Favre-saga dragged deeper into the summer than necessary, and it was a distraction the Packers couldn't overcome.

One positive, though, was the progress Rodgers showed. Rodgers was far from perfect during that 6–10 campaign, but he entered the season just 25 years old and proved he was capable of handling the position for years to come.

"I just think Aaron Rodgers today has more credibility with his teammates and probably with the media and the fan base," McCarthy said. "I don't think anybody ever questioned whether Aaron Rodgers could be a top-flight quarterback if you watched him practice every day, and that's always the biggest hurdle you have to overcome as any player, particularly at the quarterback position. Can you transfer that to the playing field, and I think that's something that Aaron can really draw from his experience this past year is how consistent that he was as a first-year starter."

Many Packers also seemed genuinely excited after McCarthy overhauled his coaching staff. When the 2008 season ended, McCarthy fired two of his four coordinators, nudged a third one into retirement, and dumped five other assistant coaches. The biggest coaching addition that offseason was defensive coordinator Dom Capers, who had twice been a head coach in the league and led the Carolina Panthers to the 1996 NFC Championship Game.

The Packers then selected linebacker Clay Matthews and nose tackle B.J. Raji in what turned out to be one of Thompson's best drafts ever.

"The one thing about our business, you are either improving or you are going the other way," McCarthy said. "I'm very excited about the additions."

Green Bay was sharp on the field that summer, too, winning its first three preseason games. Perhaps the greatest chaos came in mid-August, when Favre came out of retirement—again—and signed with divisional foe Minnesota. Twelve months earlier, that type of news would have likely thrown Rodgers off his game. But just days after the announcement, Rodgers lit up the Buffalo Bills and posted a 151.6 passer rating during an easy Packers' preseason win.

"He's got a year under his belt. I think he feels more comfortable every day," Packers running back Ryan Grant said of Rodgers. "I think if you ask him, he's on the same page with all the guys. That's been big for us."

Rodgers was extremely big that entire summer and finished with a passer rating of 147.9. He was quick

Aaron Rodgers was still in need of a signature win when the 2009 season started. He got it in the opener, rallying the Packers past archrival Chicago.

"THE ONE THING ABOUT OUR BUSINESS, YOU ARE EITHER IMPROVING OR YOU ARE GOING THE OTHER WAY. —Mike McCarthy"

with his reads, dead-on with his accuracy, and commanding in the huddle.

"He's in sync right now," McCarthy said. "You have to keep working every day to keep that, but he's had a good preseason." The regular-season opener against Chicago was just days away. And Rodgers and the Packers couldn't wait.

It had been a quiet summer, a productive summer. Rodgers and the offense had sizzled. Capers' defense had been greatly improved. And the Packers were anxious to show their 2008 season was an aberration, not the norm.

"I'm not a predictor," Packers general manager Ted Thompson said. "I don't do that. I don't want to put up any bulletin-board stuff. I do think this is a good group of guys, and I think it's a good team, and if we play well I think we'll have a chance to win. What that means I don't know.

"Every year is a new year. I do think, especially our first group, has played very well in the preseason. That is preseason, but there is a confident air in our locker room, and I think our guys think that we can hold our own against most people."

Lovie Smith, Jay Cutler, Brian Urlacher, and the Chicago Bears were first up in 2009. The Packers were about to discover exactly what they had.

. . . .

As the 2009 season kicked off, there was one area that bothered Rodgers more than any other: close games. During Rodgers' first season as a starter, the Packers went 0–7 in games decided by four points or less. And eight different times, Rodgers had a chance

to pull out a game in the final five minutes and failed each time.

"That bothers me a lot," Rodgers said shortly before the season began. "I want to fix that."

One game into the 2009 campaign, Rodgers was well on his way to repairing it. During Green Bay's season-opener with Chicago, Rodgers came up huge late in a game for the first time in his Packers career. Rodgers hit wideout Greg Jennings with a 50-yard touchdown pass with 1:11 left to lift Green Bay past Chicago, 21–15.

"I don't think I ever lost confidence in myself or my abilities [in 2008], but when you have some struggles and you make some throws you want back late in games, it's good to start a season out and be in a situation where you're called upon and expected to perform late in the game," Rodgers said afterward. "To be able to, in crunch time when it was needed, to come up with a big throw and get [the ball to] our playmaker Greg [Jennings] was very important for myself and also for our team."

Rodgers and Green Bay's offense never could get going against a fired-up Bears defense that night. But years from now, all anyone will remember from this thriller was that Rodgers delivered what was arguably his biggest moment as a Packer.

When Rodgers stepped on the field with 2:35 left, his confidence couldn't have been particularly high. The Packers trailed the Bears, 15–13. Green Bay had just 156 yards of total offense and only three points in the second half.

Green Bay began at its own 28-yard line, and four plays later, it faced a third-and-1 from midfield.

Aaron Rodgers launched his 2009 campaign after another terrific preseason, finishing with a lights-out 147.9 passer rating in the exhibition games.

McCarthy called for a Ryan Grant running play, but when Jennings lined up in the wrong spot, the Packers had to call timeout.

"It was my fault," Jennings said. "I actually designed that, to line up on the wrong side of the field so that we could go for the gold. And it got it done for us."

After the timeout, the Bears were expecting run and brought an eighth man into the box with safety Al Afalava. Rodgers ran play-action, and his first option was to tight end Donald Lee on a wheel route. Rodgers looked right to Lee, which held safety Kevin Payne in place. Jennings, who lined up on the far left, raced past cornerback Nathan Vasher.

Rodgers, who was sacked four times and hit nine others, had terrific protection on this play and lofted a perfect pass. Jennings caught it in stride at the 14 and waltzed in with the game-winner.

"I just told the guys, 'Hey, just give me one drive,'" Rodgers said of the game-winning march. "Up front, I went to the linemen and said, 'Hey, let's just protect this one drive. Give me some time, and we're going to go down and score.'"

While that provided a terrific start to the season, the first quarter of the year proved choppy. Green Bay dropped two of its next three games, including a 30–23 loss at Minnesota on Monday Night Football. That was the first meeting between Favre and Rodgers, and on that night, Favre got the best of his former understudy. Favre also got revenge on Packers general manager Ted Thompson, the man who chose Rodgers over Favre in the summer of 2007.

"I just did what I was expected to do today," Favre said afterward.

And how. Favre orchestrated four drives that went deep into Green Bay territory. And on all four, Favre's Vikings left with touchdowns. Rodgers and the Packers weren't nearly as successful. On three different occasions, Rodgers led the Packers into scoring range. Rodgers fumbled once, threw an interception, and the Packers were also stopped on downs. Three trips. Zero points.

"To have three possessions where you are in their territory and come away with zero points ... two of them were directly related to mistakes by myself, it's disappointing," Rodgers said.

Rodgers finished the night with a career-high 384 yards, a pair of touchdowns, and had a passer rating of 110.6. On paper, those statistics were comparable to Favre's (271 yards, 3 TDs, 135.3 passer rating).

The difference, though, was that Favre and the Vikings made the most of their chances, while Rodgers and the Packers couldn't.

"You can't have it," McCarthy said of the turnovers. "They took points off the board."

Green Bay bounced back with consecutive wins over NFL doormats Detroit and Cleveland by a combined score of 57–3 and improved to 4–2. But really, that was simply window dressing for the Packers' November 1 game vs. Minnesota. Brett Favre was coming back to Lambeau Field. Arguably the largest regular-season game in franchise history was just around the corner.

· ·

The Packers were trying to treat Favre's return like it was just another game. Same routine. Same preparation. Same everything. Weeks later, many admitted they were simply fooling themselves.

"We were so tight for that game...and really the whole time leading up to it," Packers defensive end Cullen Jenkins said. "That whole week before Brett came back was really tense."

It showed. During the summer of discontent in 2008, Favre said he wanted to "stick it" to Packers general manager Ted Thompson. In his return to Lambeau Field—the place he'd given Green Bay fans 16 years' worth of mostly terrific memories—Favre did exactly that.

Favre was surgeon-like, carving up Green Bay's secondary with remarkable precision and accuracy and leading the Vikings to a critical 38–26 win. Favre threw four touchdown passes for the 21st time in his career, which tied him with Dan Marino for the most in NFL history, and posted a lights-out passer rating of 128.6.

"Am I pleased with the way these two games have turned out? Absolutely," Favre said of defeating Green Bay twice. "It had nothing to do with trying to prove myself to anyone. I still have a passion for it. It's a little bit tougher to get up and bounce back, but my arm feels great. My mind is in a good place, the team has welcomed me in, and really all the other stuff doesn't matter. I know it makes for a good story. But I'm glad it's over, I'm glad we won both, but I'm not going to sit here and throw any daggers."

In Favre's first two games against Green Bay, he went 41-of-59 for 515 yards, threw seven touchdowns, had no interceptions, and finished with a passer rating of 135.9. Most importantly, Minnesota improved to 7–1 and swept the season series against the Packers (4–3).

"We talked a little bit about not doing too much," Vikings coach Brad Childress said. "You have a tendency to do too much sometimes, and I thought he did just about what he needed to do. He didn't get too creative or try to rig anything up. I just thought he kept it in body, didn't get out of body."

In the Packers' locker room, things were much more bleak. Green Bay's hopes at an NFC North title had taken a serious hit. The Packers had struggled for the second time in four weeks against an elite team. And Green Bay's confidence had undoubtedly taken a blow.

Brett Favre and his Vikings got the better of Aaron Rodgers and the Packers in their first meeting. Minnesota prevailed 30–23 in a Monday night contest at the Metrodome.

> ## "I HATE LOSING TO WHOEVER'S AT QUARTERBACK FOR THEM. I HATE LOSING TO THE VIKINGS ESPECIALLY. (THEY'RE) DIVISION RIVALS (AND WE) DON'T LIKE THOSE (LOSSES) AT HOME. —Aaron Rodgers

"I hate losing to whoever's at quarterback for them," Rodgers said. "I hate losing to the Vikings, especially. [They're] division rivals [and we] don't like those [losses] at home."

Rodgers had a rough first half, going 5-of-11 for 38 yards with a 54.4 passer rating. Overall, Green Bay managed just 47 net yards in the half, its fewest since a 31–10 loss in Denver on October 17, 1999. Not surprisingly, the Packers were in a 17–3 hole.

"We weren't in a rhythm," Rodgers said of Green Bay's first-half struggles. "I think that's the first thing. That was due to a lack of execution."

Rodgers and the Packers did get rolling after halftime. In fact, Green Bay scored on four straight possessions—three touchdowns and one field goal—to close to within 31–26. The Packers abandoned their putrid rushing game and let Rodgers wing it around against Minnesota's overmatched secondary. And Rodgers had a second-half passer rating of 128.3 after completing 21 of 30 attempts for 249 yards, three touchdowns, and no interceptions.

"I started hitting guys that were open," Rodgers said. "The first half I struggled, missed a couple throws I should have hit. When we get into a rhythm on offense, we're tough to stop."

Trailing 31–26 with 8:13 left, Rodgers and the Packers took over at their own 19. Just two plays later, the Packers had marched to Minnesota's 28.

But on second-and-3, Rodgers took his sixth sack of the game, losing five yards on the play. Rodgers then threw incomplete on third down, and Mason Crosby proceeded to miss a 51-yard field goal.

Brett Favre and the Vikings reclaimed the ball—and quickly regained all momentum. On Minnesota's first play, Favre hit Adrian Peterson for 44 yards on a screen pass. Then two plays later, Favre hummed a 16-yard TD pass to Bernard Berrian. Ball game.

Again, doubts about Rodgers' ability to deliver in the clutch persisted.

"You look at everything that evolves around your football team, and Aaron is part of the solution," Packers coach Mike McCarthy said. "There is no doubt about it. He is definitely one of the positives, but he has things he needs to work on too, just like every member of our football team."

The Packers figured to get well the following week with a trip to Tampa Bay to face the 0–7 Buccaneers. Green Bay entered the game as a 10-point favorite, but they played arguably their worst game of the McCarthy era and fell to hapless Tampa Bay, 38–28.

"I've been asked about the rebound from Minnesota. Hell, we have to rebound from Tampa Bay," McCarthy said. "We've had two tough losses in a row here, and we need to handle the adversity that's in front of us. We didn't handle the adversity of the way the game went up and down as a team, and that starts with me."

Rodgers was unable to rally the Packers from a big deficit against visiting Minnesota during their second 2009 meeting. Like the earlier game, Favre and the Vikings prevailed, this time 38–26.

The adversity on the field was nothing, though, compared to the difficulties off of it. One day after the brutal loss, the Packers' offense gathered to clear the air—and clear the air they did.

"There were some deep-seated emotions in that room that needed to get out—that guys were holding in," Rodgers said. "It was great. There were a lot of harsh words said, but at the end of the day, we moved on together.

"A lot of times when there is strife on a team it can get out in the wrong way—guys talking in the media on their own or behind the scenes—but we sat in the room as an offense and said, 'What are the main issues here?' Myself, Donald [Driver], and different guys spoke up, and we got our issues on the table and moved forward as a team. It wasn't a divided locker room. We stayed together, talked about our problems, and moved forward together."

The Packers were moving forward with a disappointing 4–4 record. With a brutal second-half schedule still looming, much of Packer Nation was wondering if 2009 would be another lost year.

. . . .

The following week, Dallas came to Lambeau Field winners of four straight games and leading the NFC East with a 6–2 mark. Green Bay's season, meanwhile, was hanging by a string. The Packers entered as a 3-point underdog on their own field, knowing another loss might keep them from the postseason.

"The importance and urgency has to increase," McCarthy said.

To the surprise of many, it did. Rodgers keyed a pair of huge fourth-quarter touchdown drives, running for one score and throwing for another. Green Bay held Dallas to season-lows in rushing yards (61) and total yards (278). And the Packers exited with a critical 17–7 victory.

"It was a big win for us definitely," Rodgers said afterward. "We knew (being) 4–4 (and) playing a very good team, it was an important time in our season to get back in this race. I think a lot of people were thinking this was going to be the end of the road for us and going to be a turning point for the negative for us this season. But it was a big win for our team."

It sure was. Since the start of the 2008 season, Green Bay had been 10–14 and had defeated only two teams with winning records. But this was arguably Green Bay's most impressive win under Rodgers.

"We said all week, if we want this season to turn out the way we think it should, we have to make a run, and it needs to start this week," fullback John Kuhn said. "It can't start next week, it can't start on Thanksgiving [against Detroit], and it can't start in December. It has to start now. This is just a starting point, though. It isn't anything special. We're going to enjoy the win for a day or two, then get right back at it."

Boy, did they ever. The Dallas game started a five-game winning streak that saw Green Bay climb to 9–4, jump right back into the playoff hunt, and silence many that doubted Rodgers and the Packers.

"There are a lot of positive aspects and variables of our football team," McCarthy said. "The most important thing is those positive things, we need them to show up every week, and we need to continue to improve."

The Packers—and Rodgers—were both riding high. Green Bay followed its win over Dallas with a 30–24 victory over San Francisco. Rodgers was extremely sharp that day, going 32-of-45 with two TD passes—including a 64-yarder to Greg Jennings.

The Packers then drilled Detroit, 34–12, on Thanksgiving. Rodgers again had a huge day with three TD passes, 348 passing yards, and no interceptions.

"Consistent," McCarthy said of Rodgers. "He's doing a very good job of running the offense, not taking chances. I think the pass protection has improved week to week, and he's just doing a great job of running the offense. We've been playing at a high level here on offense."

That didn't change the following week against a terrific Baltimore defense. Rodgers threw three touchdowns—including two to standout tight end Jermichael Finley—and the Packers upended the Ravens, 27–14.

"I WOULD CLEARLY SAY THAT AARON RODGERS HAS FALLEN INTO THE CLASSIFICATION OF A FRANCHISE QUARTERBACK."
—Mike McCarthy

The following week, Green Bay ventured south to face archrival Chicago. The Bears had lost four of five, were 5–7 overall and virtually eliminated from postseason play. But nothing is ever easy when these teams meet, and it wasn't on this day either.

The Packers trailed, 14–13, in the fourth quarter when Nick Collins intercepted Chicago's Jay Cutler and returned the pick to the Bears' 11-yard line. Two plays later, Ryan Grant banged in, and the Packers eventually escaped with a 21–14 win. The Packers were now 9–4, and their five-game winning streak was their third-longest of the decade. Capers' defense was improving by the week. Rodgers had the offense humming along.

There were still three games remaining. But Rodgers had certainly won over his head coach.

"I would clearly say that Aaron Rodgers has fallen into the classification of a franchise quarterback," McCarthy said. "He has played at that level. I know it's only been a year and a half or a year and three-quarters. I think he's definitely at that level of play, so I just think that in itself tells you how we feel about him and his value to our football team."

The following week, the Packers saw a quarterback just as deadly: Pittsburgh's Ben Roethlisberger. Little did anyone know, but it was a prelude of things to come. On a cold December day in Pittsburgh, Rodgers and Roethlisberger engaged in classic shootout.

Rodgers was brilliant throughout, throwing for 383 yards, three touchdowns, and rushing for a fourth score. In fact, Rodgers was so deadly that after the Steelers took a 30–28 lead with four minutes left,

Pittsburgh coach Mike Tomlin made the unusual decision to try an onside kick.

"In the latter part of the fourth quarter, I felt that both offenses were capable of moving the football," Tomlin said. "We had 30 minutes of evidence to show they could also drive the ball on us. That's why we took the risk when we did."

It didn't pay off, as Pittsburgh's onside kick went just nine yards. Then Rodgers hit James Jones with a 24-yard TD pass with 2:06 remaining to put the Packers back ahead, 36–30. Pittsburgh still had two minutes left, though, which was a lifetime in this thriller. And on the final play of the game, Roethlisberger hit Mike Wallace in the left corner of the end zone for a 19-yard TD and a 37–36 Steelers win.

"You lose on a last-second play, with a spectacular throw and catch, it's tough," Packers linebacker Clay Matthews said. "Hindsight's always 20-20, but we knew what we were getting ourselves into. It was a dogfight."

Roethlisberger finished with a remarkable 503 passing yards, the most ever by a Pittsburgh quarterback. The five-game winning streak was over. And the Packers still had some work to do to earn a playoff spot.

But the fact that Green Bay had gone to Pittsburgh and played the defending Super Bowl champs toe-to-toe was highly encouraging.

"We came up one play short, and it will be corrected tomorrow," McCarthy said afterward. "I'm sure there will be a number of opportunities where we could've probably made one play. I think this is classic

December football. It came down to the last play of the game, and we didn't get it done."

But one week later, Rodgers and the Packers picked up right where they'd left off. Green Bay rolled up 417 yards of total offense and routed visiting Seattle, 48–10. When Carolina defeated the New York Giants that day, the Packers had clinched their first playoff berth since Favre left. And afterward, several players took a lap around Lambeau Field to acknowledge the fans.

Green Bay followed that with a 33–7 beatdown of host Arizona and finished the regular season 11–5. The Cardinals took a cautious approach to the game and rested many of their key players, knowing they were likely to face Green Bay in the first round of the playoffs. The Packers, meanwhile, tried to add to the momentum they'd established in the second half of the season—something they accomplished with relative ease.

"It's an impressive body of work, the second half of the season," McCarthy said. "That's the truth, that's the reality, and that has been acknowledged. Also, it's our responsibility as coaches to keep driving this football team. They're fun to coach. They still have a lot of work in front of them. I still see the opportunity to improve....We've been playing really good football here the second half of the season."

The Packers finished the regular season by winning seven of their final eight games. They finished the year ranked No. 2 in total defense and No. 6 in total offense. And Rodgers was one of four Packers named to the Pro Bowl.

"We're doing a lot of good things right now, and we want to be sure not to take our foot off the gas," left guard Daryn Colledge said. "Playoffs are playoffs, and you can throw the records out once we get to that. So I think everything's wide open once we get to that."

The fifth-seeded Packers drew fourth-seeded Arizona in the opening round. Although the Cardinals had won the NFC 12 months earlier, McCarthy and the Packers were extremely confident. In fact, internally,

many Packers believed they were ready to win a Super Bowl.

"As we talk as a football team, our goal of winning the world championship is right in front of us," McCarthy said. "And that's all you can ask for, is opportunities. You have to get into the playoffs to accomplish that. We're going to be a road warrior mentality as we plan for that.

"We're excited about qualifying for the playoffs, but you know we need to continue to play the way we're playing. I'm excited about the momentum and the progress we've made as a football team, and we still have an opportunity to improve."

• •

In two short years as an NFL starter, Rodgers had quarterbacked some awfully big games. Rodgers faced former teammate Brett Favre and the Minnesota Vikings twice in 2009. He outdueled Tony Romo and Dallas in a critical contest in mid-November that helped the Packers turn around their season. Rodgers won his first-ever start on a Monday night against Minnesota and also spearheaded an impressive 2008 win against Peyton Manning and Indianapolis.

But those games paled in comparison to what was coming. Kurt Warner, Larry Fitzgerald, and an Arizona Cardinals team that came within seconds of winning the Super Bowl XLIII were on deck. Rodgers was the first quarterback not named Brett Favre to guide the Packers into the postseason since Lynn Dickey in 1982. And the Packers felt they had everything going for them.

"Anything can happen," Rodgers said. "Like Kevin Garnett said, 'Anything's possible.' We're very excited about the opportunity to get to the second season. We realize in order to get where we want to go we're going to have to win on the road. But I think you look at Coach McCarthy's record since he's been here, and we've had a pretty good road record.

"The guys realize their responsibilities when we go on the road, and we like our chances. We like the way we're playing. We're peaking at the right time...

As the 2009 postseason arrived, Aaron Rodgers and the Packers were red hot, with wins in seven of their last eight games.

"That's probably one of the best games ever played in the playoffs," Cardinals coach Ken Whisenhunt said afterward.

Aside from the ending, the Packers might have agreed. Old-pro Warner, who would retire at the end of the season, destroyed Green Bay's overmatched secondary throughout. Warner completed a remarkable 29 of 33 passes (87.9 percent) for 379 yards and five touchdowns and no interceptions.

"It was just one of those games where I felt great," Warner said. "I felt like I was seeing everything well, and it accumulates to 51 points."

Rodgers was nearly as good, setting a Packers postseason record with 423 passing yards. Rodgers also threw four touchdowns and ran for one. In the end, though, Green Bay's defense didn't do nearly enough for the Packers to advance. And Rodgers game-ending turnover proved fatal.

"You go back to Pittsburgh," Packers cornerback Charles Woodson said after the loss to Arizona. "Similar type of offense, and they were able to move the ball up and down the field the same way, made big plays when they needed to, and we find ourselves not being able to get off the field."

Arizona's defense had to feel the same way as Rodgers and Warner took turns lighting up the scoreboard. Rodgers and the Packers struggled early, falling behind 17–0 and later 31–10. But Rodgers led the Packers to seven straight scoring drives—six touchdowns and a field goal—to end regulation tied at 45.

"I started very slowly and didn't make a lot of good plays early on to get us into position to win," Rodgers

and excited about the possibilities that await us in that second season."

Veteran wideout Donald Driver agreed.

"We're in great hands with [Rodgers]," he said. "There hasn't been too much that's bothered him so far, so I don't know why it would be anything different now. I'll take my chances with [Rodgers] any day of the week."

In most instances, that bet would have paid off. But in a memorable wild-card game, Arizona's Warner was slightly more deadly than Rodgers, and the Cardinals won a classic, 51–45, in overtime.

Unfortunately for Rodgers and the Packers, the game ended when Rodgers held the ball too long and was stripped by Arizona's Michael Adams. Karlos Dansby recovered the fumble and went 17 yards for a touchdown that gave the Cardinals a victory in the highest-scoring postseason game in NFL history.

Aaron Rodgers and the Green Bay Packers got off to a rough start against the Arizona Cardinals in their 2009 NFC wild-card game. Green Bay fell behind by 21 points on two different occasions.

said. "We were able to get on a roll there in the second half. Unfortunately, we couldn't make enough plays to win."

Rodgers made a remarkable amount of plays, though, in his first playoff start. Early in the third quarter, Rodgers fired a 6-yard TD to Greg Jennings and an 11-yard scoring strike to Jordy Nelson within 3 minutes to pull the Packers to within 31–24. After the Cardinals answered back, Rodgers engineered scoring drives of 80 and 67 yards to tie the game at 38. It was the first time the game had been tied since the opening minutes.

Warner responded with a 17-yard TD pass to Steve Breaston to put the Cardinals back ahead, 45–38. But Rodgers never flinched and threw an 11-yard TD pass to Spencer Havner to force overtime.

"If you had come in this morning and told me our offense would score 45 points," defensive end Cullen Jenkins said, "I'd be like, 'Yeah, we're going to win.'"

When the Packers won the coin toss to start overtime, they had to feel like a win was in the cards. But on the first play of overtime, Rodgers missed a wide-open Jennings on what would have been an 80-yard, game-winning TD. Two plays later, he was sacked, fumbled, and Dansby's return ended Green Bay's year. Replays showed that Adams grabbed Rodgers' face mask on the sack and strip. But no flag was thrown, and the Packers' season was over just like that.

"I think anytime you're sitting around waiting on calls to win football games, you're in a mode of excuses," McCarthy said. "The way the game ended, you don't want it to come down to an officiating call. Nobody wants that. You want it to be about player productivity. There was a lot of productivity in that football game, especially from an offensive standpoint. But I'm not going to sit here and try to discredit Arizona's victory by no means, because it really doesn't do any good."

Despite the disappointing end, there was plenty of good for Rodgers and the Packers in 2009. And in many ways, it set the Packers up for much of their 2010 success. Rodgers had a breakout year, finishing fourth in the NFL in passer rating (103.2), passing

Aaron Rodgers is hit in overtime by Cardinals cornerback Michael Adams, causing a fumble that Arizona recovered and returned for the winning touchdown in the NFC wild-card Game.

yards (4,434), and touchdowns (30). He also threw just seven interceptions, and his interception percentage of 1.3 ranked first in football.

Rodgers also became the first quarterback in league history to eclipse more than 4,000 passing yards in each of his first two years as a starter. And Rodgers' 4,434 passing yards were second in team history, behind only Lynn Dickey's 4,458 in 1983. More importantly, though, Green Bay won 11 games after winning just six the previous campaign.

"I think Aaron has had a very good year," McCarthy said of Rodgers. "I don't think there's [any] doubt about that. When you go win it all, I think that's when you start talking about great seasons. But he was definitely a very bright positive for our football team, both on the field and in the locker room, and we feel very good about that as an organization. I definitely felt that he had a very, very good year."

Rodgers didn't throw an interception in 12 of his 16 games, breaking the old mark of 11 held by Bart Starr in 1964. Rodgers also punished defenses with his feet. His 316 rushing yards were the second-most in football by a quarterback. He also scored five rushing touchdowns, the most by a Packer quarterback since Don Majkowski also had five in 1989.

In addition, third down was also a magical one for Rodgers. On that down alone, Rodgers had a 133.5 passer rating, threw 14 TDs, and had no interceptions. Rodgers' 1,710 passing yards on third down were also the most since the stat was originated in 1991.

"Aaron Rodgers is a Pro Bowl quarterback, and that's the facts," McCarthy said. "Trust me, I fully understand the greatness of Brett Favre, and I had the opportunity to be part of his career, and he deserves everything that comes his way.

"But this is the beginning of potentially another great career at quarterback here in Green Bay, and [fans] should embrace it. That would be my suggestion if there is any doubt. He's putting up Pro Bowl numbers in both of his seasons. It does come down to winning, winning is important, but he's put together two quality seasons so far."

Rodgers also appeared to turn a corner sometime around the Dallas game. He started making quicker decisions, and instead of typically playing things safe, he tried making plays each week that only the NFL's elite are capable of. Rodgers was sacked 37 times in the first eight games of the year, with many of those being his fault. But Rodgers showed dramatic improvement in the second half of the year when he was sacked just 13 times in the final eight games.

"I'm very impressed," Packers cornerback Charles Woodson said of Rodgers. "The numbers speak for themselves, to go back-to-back seasons with 4,000 yards. I don't know too many quarterbacks that have gone through the transition that he had to go through when Brett left the team.

"For him to go through that this year, to go through the numerous amount of sacks that he has gone through, and taking a lot of heat for supposedly holding the football too long, and that sort of thing. He comes to work every day, prepares every day like a winning quarterback, and then on Sundays he shows up. Again, he keeps getting up off the ground and making plays for this team. There is not enough that can be said about what he has done this year."

Of course, the disappointing conclusion would linger with Green Bay's players throughout a long off-season. And when 2010 rolled around, the Packers insisted they'd be hungrier than ever.

"This is just going to make myself and these guys want it that much more," Rodgers said of the loss to Arizona. "It might not look like we came that close, but we still feel like we were close to achieving all the goals we set forth at the beginning of the season."

Indeed they were.

Little did anyone know it, but 12 months later those goals would be met. ∎

Despite his phenomenal second-half performance against the Cardinals, Rodgers' second season as starter ended in frustration when the Packers fell in the first round of the playoffs.

2010: REGULAR SEASON ROLLER-COASTER

Bold. Brash. Bombastic. That's how the 2010 Packers were going to operate. When the Packers concluded their offseason program in late June, they lightened the mood by holding a home run hitting contest. Rookie offensive tackle Bryan Bulaga won the event, and for his efforts, was presented a broken-down car. While many chuckled at Bulaga's new vehicle, the message on the car was no laughing matter. On the driver's side, it read: "To Super Bowl—Dallas."

"I definitely think we're positioned to do that," veteran wideout Donald Driver said. "Super Bowl's the goal, and I don't think we're going to be shy about saying it."

Later that summer, Rodgers and several of his teammates showed up at the annual Welcome Back Packers Luncheon. They did so wearing cowboy hats and bolo ties. By all accounts, the stunt was Rodgers' idea. The message was also crystal clear: Green Bay's goal was to finish its season in Arlington, Texas, home of Super Bowl XLV.

"I have every intention and belief that we have the capability of winning the Super Bowl," Packers coach Mike McCarthy said. "Every decision that we make toward our football team, toward our program, toward our environment is always trying to improve our football team."

As the 2010 season dawned, the Packers were everybody's darlings. Several national publications had picked Green Bay to win the Super Bowl, even though it hadn't won a playoff game in the post-Favre era. The Packers, themselves, were doing nothing to quiet the noise.

"I just had our team meeting, and we talked about winning the Super Bowl," McCarthy said the day before training camp began. "We talked about where it is played at and the relevance of our team meeting room.

"The only team pictures that are in that room are the team pictures of the world champions of the Green Bay Packers. Everything that we have done throughout the offseason and everything that we'll do starting tomorrow will be taking a step to being the next team up on that wall. That's our goal."

Rodgers was also a hot pick for MVP honors after another stellar preseason. In three outings that summer, Rodgers threw for six touchdowns, no interceptions, and posted a ridiculous passer rating of 141.2.

"It's honestly never entered my thought process," Rodgers said of the MVP talk. "You know, the awards and the predictions and stuff, really, I think that's preseason fodder. Just stuff to chew on while the games may not be as meaningful. But once we get into the everyday grind of the season, guys are just focused on that week."

As the season began, there were several striking parallels to Green Bay's 1996 team—the last Packers squad to win a Super Bowl. Rodgers was 26 when the season began, the same age Brett Favre was at the start

Aaron Rodgers had another terrific preseason in 2010 and became a hot pick for MVP honors.

> ## I HAVE EVERY INTENTION AND BELIEF THAT WE HAVE THE CAPABILITY OF WINNING THE SUPER BOWL. —Mike McCarthy

of 1996. Both players were also beginning their sixth NFL season. Ted Thompson was 57 at the start of the 2010 season and beginning his sixth year as Green Bay's general manager. Back in 1996, Ron Wolf was 57 and beginning his fifth full season as the Packers' GM.

Finally, McCarthy was 46 when the 2010 season opened and starting his fifth year as the Packers' head coach. In 1996, Mike Holmgren, 48, was also beginning his fifth year as the Packers' head coach.

"That is crazy," Packers wideout Jordy Nelson said. "I know you guys can do a lot with stats, but that one is pretty wild."

Not everyone was buying into the hype, though, including some members of Green Bay's last Super Bowl team. The Packers of 1996 were built through a variety of ways: the NFL Draft, free agency, trades, etc. But Thompson never dabbled much in free agency, choosing instead to build his roster almost entirely through the NFL Draft and then develop talent internally. As the season began, many from the old guard wondered exactly how far Thompson could eventually take this franchise.

"You have to make a decision as a general manager: do you want to win championships or do you want to win games?" asked former safety LeRoy Butler, who made four Pro Bowls during his 12-year Packer career. "Ted's going to win games because of Aaron [Rodgers] and because he drafts well. But unless he changes his philosophy when it comes to free agency, it's going to be hard to win championships.

"Right now, the gap between Minnesota and the Packers is huge if Brett [Favre] comes back. How are the Packers going to close that gap? By just drafting a bunch of young guys? The thing is, Ted doesn't believe in getting a 30-year-old veteran to help you do that. He wants to fill his holes with young guys."

When the 1995 Packers had lost in the NFC Championship Game at Dallas, Wolf added free agents such as defensive tackle Santana Dotson, kick returner Desmond Howard, wideout Don Beebe, left tackle Bruce Wilkerson, and linebacker Ron Cox, then also traded for safety Eugene Robinson. Those moves helped get the Packers over the hump the following season.

While the prospects for Green Bay's 2010 season were extremely bright, Thompson had been quiet the entire offseason. And many wondered if his philosophy could ever take the Packers to the promised land.

"I know we added some veterans to help us get over the hump," former Packers wideout Robert Brooks said. "But if you've got players who can step in and play, it doesn't matter if they're rookies or if they've been around a long time. Me personally, I'm really excited about this Packers team coming up."

So were the Packers themselves. With the season-opener in Philadelphia just days away, the Packers were bringing back 21 of 22 preferred starters. Rodgers' combination of physical skills and knowledge of the offense was better than ever. Green Bay's young talent was blossoming. And McCarthy had the total backing of the locker room.

Big things appeared in store.

"We talked about the Super Bowl expectations, we set our goals for the season on the first day of training

camp," McCarthy said. "I like the confidence of our team, but we're at the starting line."

Of what promised to be one remarkable journey.

. . . .

As the 2010 season opened, Green Bay's star power matched any in football. Jermichael Finley was coming off a season in which his 55 catches were the second-most in team history by a tight end. Finley also finished the year with a memorable 159-yard effort in the playoff loss to Arizona.

The wide receiver quartet of Greg Jennings, Donald Driver, Jordy Nelson, and James Jones matched any in football. Running back Ryan Grant, one of the game's more underappreciated players, had 11 TDs in 2009 and nearly 2,500 rushing yards over the last two seasons.

Cornerback Charles Woodson was the NFL's reigning defensive MVP. Linebacker Clay Matthews set a franchise rookie record with 10 sacks during his first

year, and safety Nick Collins had played in consecutive Pro Bowls.

But with Rodgers beginning his sixth season—and third as the starter—the Packers were officially his team. And like Lambeau, Hutson, Lombardi, Starr, and Favre before him, Rodgers was now the face of the Packers.

"It's not something I think about a whole lot," Rodgers said. "I realize my position on this team as quarterback kind of warrants some of that stuff. But as far as a responsibility to that, I am definitely OK with that."

The Packers were certainly okay with it, as well. Green Bay opened the 2010 season at Philadelphia—a team going through a similar transition to what the Packers endured in 2008. The Eagles had parted ways with veteran quarterback Donovan McNabb that off-season and were turning the reins over to young Kevin Kolb. The situation mirrored that of Green Bay's move from Favre to Rodgers two years earlier.

As the 2010 season began, Aaron Rodgers had won over most of the Green Bay Packers fan base.

"We've definitely conversed more than once in the last few months," Rodgers said of he and Kolb. "He reached out to me and wanted my number. That was a no-brainer for me. I was just honored that he wanted to seek my input-slash-advice.

"I'm definitely a fan of his. Having been in a similar situation, he's definitely a guy I'm pulling for 15 weeks out of the season. He's a very talented guy. I have no doubt he's going to make a very smooth transition."

Well, not quite. Kolb struggled early, then was knocked out of the game after suffering a concussion on a sack from Matthews. Michael Vick came in, was dynamic, and never relinquished the starting job.

Despite Vick's best efforts, the Packers were too much for the Eagles.

Green Bay built a 27–10 lead behind two Rodgers' TD passes and a TD run from John Kuhn. The Packers then held on as Vick mounted a furious fourth-quarter rally and won in Philadelphia for the first time since 1962, 27–20.

"I thought it was a very gutty performance on both sides of the field, and we feel very fortunate to come out of here with a win," McCarthy said. "This is a tough place to play, and it's a tough football team to play against."

Green Bay didn't leave unscathed, though. Grant was lost for the year with an ankle injury, and the

Aaron Rodgers accounted for three touchdowns as the Packers routed the Buffalo Bills 34–7 and improved to 2–0.

Packers would have to move forward without their No. 1 running back.

"Ryan Grant is exactly the type of individual you want on your team and in your program, the way he goes about his business," McCarthy said. "He is a hard-working, tough guy, no-nonsense, no-excuse individual, and he is a very good teammate. So the personal angle of Ryan's injury is definitely difficult."

Fortunately for the Packers, NFL doormat Buffalo was up next, and Green Bay was able to ease into life without Grant. Matthews had three more sacks, pushing his NFL-leading total to six. Rodgers threw for 255 yards and accounted for three touchdowns as the Packers rolled to a 34–7 win.

One of the few things that didn't go right came when Rodgers scrambled for a touchdown, but was far from graceful on his Lambeau Leap.

"The guys gave me a hard time on the sideline," Rodgers said. "But I told them, 'Look, I was tired.'"

The Packers hadn't been perfect their first two games. Far from. But they were 2–0 and headed to Chicago for a first-place showdown with the undefeated Bears. Chicago had finished just 7–9 the previous season, but the Bears defense—decimated by injury in 2009—was healthy again and playing at a high level. And quarterback Jay Cutler, now in his second season in Chicago, was maturing.

"I think they are playing with a lot of confidence, very good tempo on defense," McCarthy said of the Bears. "It looks like they have been productive on offense, and their special teams has always been a challenge. We are looking for this to be a heck of a football game on Monday night."

It was. It just wasn't the outcome Green Bay hoped for. The Packers set a new team record with 18 penalties. Chicago's Devin Hester returned a punt 62 yards for a touchdown, his first return for a score in three years. And Packers wideout James Jones had a critical late-game fumble that set up Chicago's Robbie Gould for a chip shot field goal that gave the Bears a 20–17 win.

"It was an uncharacteristic game on offense for us, well, just as a team," Rodgers said. "Way too many penalties."

Rodgers was sharp, completing 34 of 45 passes for 316 yards and accounting for two touchdowns. But the penalties, two Green Bay turnovers, and rotten special teams play were too much to overcome.

"We'll take a look at the film, but [18] penalties, that doesn't cut it," McCarthy said. "You can't play football like that."

Despite this Rodgers touchdown, Green Bay self-destructed in its first meeting against the Bears, committing a record 18 penalties en route to a 20–17 loss.

"WE'RE NOT PLAYING CHAMPIONSHIP FOOTBALL RIGHT NOW.... BUT THERE'S A LOT OF SEASON LEFT. —Donald Lee

Green Bay wasn't much better the following week, but they held off Detroit for a 28–26 win. The Packers were at the quarter pole in their season and were 3–1 overall. But Green Bay wasn't playing at nearly the same level it had all summer, and that Super Bowl talk had certainly quieted.

"There's a lot of things we've got to clean up and get better at," said linebacker Brady Poppinga. "I don't think anyone's totally happy with how we're playing right now. But we are 3–1. That's a good thing."

Green Bay's special teams, a bugaboo for years, continued to spring leaks. The running game had yet to find its legs without Grant. And the defense allowed 331 passing yards to Lions career backup Shaun Hill. The offense did just enough, though, as Rodgers threw first-half touchdowns to Driver, Finley, and Jennings, and the Packers survived a late Detroit surge.

The biggest drawback, though, was injuries. The Packers lost veteran right tackle Mark Tauscher (shoulder), inside linebacker Nick Barnett (wrist), and rookie safety Morgan Burnett (ACL) in this game, and all three didn't play again in 2010.

"We're not playing championship football right now. I'd agree with that," tight end Donald Lee said. "But there's a lot of season left."

Unfortunately for the Packers, their season was about to get worse before it got better. Green Bay played arguably its worst game of the season and dropped a 16–13 overtime decision in Washington the following week. The Redskins overcame a 10-point, fourth-quarter deficit to stun Green Bay.

Injuries continued to mount, as well. Rodgers suffered a concussion in the loss, while both Finley (knee), defensive end Mike Neal (shoulder), and special teams ace Derrick Martin (knee) suffered season-ending injuries.

"There is no 'woe is me' here," McCarthy proclaimed after the Redskins loss. "This is the National Football League. It's a dynamic business. Not at the extent of getting players hurt, I like where we are at as a team. I think this is an excellent opportunity for us to show what we are about. I know there is probably doubt outside the room."

That was true, and that doubt got even greater when the Packers dropped a 23–20 overtime decision to Miami and fell to 3–3. The Packers were now just 1–3 in 2010 in games decided by four points or less and 1–11 since Favre departed.

"We've just got to pull through and find a way to win," running back Brandon Jackson said. "I don't know how. We've just got to win. Just got to win. All I know is we have to play better. We have to run better, we have throw better, we have to catch better. We're way better than what the record says, but we are what the record says. We've just got to come out and play better for four quarters and not give an opponent a chance to come back and win the ball game."

Green Bay's defense, which was playing without Matthews, did its job and got a stop to start overtime. But the offense went three-and-out, and then punter Tim Masthay shanked a 37-yarder. Miami then had to move just 26 yards before getting a game-winning field goal.

"We're definitely not where we want to be," linebacker Desmond Bishop said. "At the same time, it's a long season, and we can definitely get it back on track.

We're competitors...and all it takes is a little tightening of some screws here and there, and I think we're going to be hitting on all cylinders and get going."

It had to happen fast. Favre and the Vikings were coming to town, and Green Bay couldn't afford a repeat of 2009 when it lost to Minnesota twice.

. . . .

Rodgers and the Packers tried to keep things as normal as possible throughout the week, saying that this was just one of 16 games on the schedule. But everyone knew it was much more than that. Beating Favre and the Vikings would definitely be overcoming a mental hurdle for Rodgers and the Packers, especially after Minnesota had recently traded for wideout Randy Moss. It wasn't easy, but Green Bay posted an impressive 28–24 win.

The Packers built a 28–17 third-quarter lead and then held on down the stretch. Favre had rallied the Vikings to within 28–24 and drove Minnesota to Green Bay's 20-yard line in the closing moments. But Favre's

fourth-down pass to the end zone for Moss was too high, and the Packers notched an enormous win.

"A loss could have been devastating," said cornerback Tramon Williams, who was in coverage on Moss on the Vikings' final offensive play. "It would have been another loss to Minnesota. Whew."

Whew is right.

It was far too early in the year to call Green Bay's win a "season saver." But there's no doubt a third straight loss would have been extremely damaging on many levels. After losing twice to Minnesota in 2009, many of the Packers admitted there was somewhat of a "hangover" effect. This was the type of narrow win that had avoided Green Bay for much of the Aaron Rodgers–Mike McCarthy era.

Doing it against Favre and the Vikings made it even sweeter.

"It was a little more special," Rodgers said. "Because of the significance of where we're at in the season, 3–3 coming in, our opponent, [a] division

By the time the 2010 regular season had ended, Aaron Rodgers had defeated Brett Favre twice and had begun to escape Favre's enormous shadow.

opponent, our biggest rival, and the close score, the way it ended. It definitely is a special night for us."

In addition, Rodgers got the best of his individual battle with Favre. Rodgers threw for two touchdowns, two interceptions, and had an 84.8 passer rating. Favre struggled and threw three interceptions, one touchdown, and posted just a 50.4 passer rating.

With Chicago starting to struggle, the Packers were again tied atop the NFC North at 4–3, while the Vikings fell to 2–4. And with every team in the NFC having lost at least twice, the conference was once again wide open.

"I think these are just the type of games you have to win if you want to be a good team," linebacker A.J. Hawk said. "We lost a couple games like this in the last couple weeks that we knew we could have had. But that's how it goes. It's a long season. We've just got to keep going. It's not really about anyone else. If we take care of our job, we'll be where we want to be. This is one tiny little step, and we're going to keep moving."

They did. Rodgers and the offense were still learning exactly how to play without Finley and Grant, two of their most vital weapons. In addition, the injuries kept piling up. Outside linebacker Brad Jones damaged his shoulder and went on injured reserve after the Minnesota game. Brady Poppinga, Jones' backup, also suffered a knee injury against Miami and went on I.R.

But the Packers were learning to overcome such adversity and finding a way to win in the process. The victory over Minnesota gave Green Bay an enormous shot of confidence and a real belief that it could turn around a season that hadn't always gone as hoped. The Packers played with a poise and coolness the following week and upset the New York Jets, 9–0.

The Jets had entered the game a six-point favorite, but Green Bay forced three turnovers and blanked Rex Ryan's bombastic bunch. New York, widely considered the AFC's top team, had been humbled on their home field, and the Packers were once again riding high.

Rodgers and the Green Bay offense struggled against the Jets in New York, but the defense was stellar in recording a 9–0 shutout.

"We love to be underdogs," Packers safety Nick Collins said. "Everybody thinks the Jets are the team to win the Super Bowl. We wanted to come in here and match their intensity and show them that we can play with anybody."

Green Bay was just getting started. One week later, with a national television audience watching, the Packers played one of their finest games in McCarthy's five-year tenure. Green Bay dominated in every facet and routed Dallas, 45–7, on Sunday Night Football.

"[The Packers] whipped us about every way you could whip somebody," said Cowboys coach Wade Phillips, who was fired the following day. "They're a good football team playing at home, and they played well, and we didn't play well at all. That's the way the game went."

Green Bay's offense finally hit its stride, as well. The Packers rolled up 415 yards of total offense, their second-highest total of the season. Green Bay had a season-high 26 first downs and converted a season-best 66.7 percent of its third downs (10-of-15).

Rodgers threw for 289 yards and three touchdowns, completed 79.4 percent of his passes and had a 131.5 passer rating, the third-highest total of his career.

Rodgers' arms and legs were too much for the Cowboys on November 7, 2010. The Packers' 45–7 rout cost Dallas coach Wade Phillips his job the next day.

Wideout James Jones set career highs in catches (eight) and yards (123). And the Packers ran for 138 yards, their second-highest total of the year.

"I think we had a good plan," said Rodgers, who had his highest passer rating of the season. "We just got into a flow early. I think I haven't played this kind of game really this season yet. I'm playing the way I feel like I'm capable of playing. It was nice to play better. It was obviously a combination of a number of things, but Mike [McCarthy] called some very high-percentage plays early in the game for me, and I feel like I really got into a rhythm early."

Green Bay was heading to its bye week with a 6–3 record and a three-game winning streak. The first stretch of the season was far more challenging than anyone would have imagined, but somehow, Rodgers and the Packers had survived.

"It gives us momentum going into the bye week," Woodson said of the dominating win. "We have some time off, which slows us down a little bit, but hopefully we come back in a couple weeks ready to go, and have that same intensity."

They did. In its first game after the bye week, Green Bay went to Minnesota to face a Vikings team on the brink of collapse. By the time things had ended, Minnesota had undoubtedly crumbled. Rodgers was virtually flawless, throwing for 301 yards and four touchdowns, including three to Jennings. Favre had another rough day, and the Packers routed their border-state rivals, 31–3.

"This has got me at a loss for words," Favre said afterward. "Disappointing would be an understatement."

One day later, Vikings owner Zigi Wilf fired head coach Brad Childress. It marked the second time in as many games that the Packers' rout of an opponent led to the dismissal of their head coach.

"We've got a foot on the gas, hands on the wheel, and we're looking straight ahead," McCarthy said.

Twelve months earlier, the Packers couldn't solve Favre and the Vikings. Now, in less than a month, Green Bay had vanquished them both twice.

The Packers were suddenly the hottest team in the NFC, thanks to a four-game winning streak in which their average margin of victory was 19.8 points. Green Bay (7–3) was tied for first place in the NFC North and on its way to Atlanta (8–2) for a shot at first place in the conference.

"We're a good football team; we always knew we were a good football team," McCarthy said. "We'll crank it up and get ready for Atlanta."

The Packers' trip to the Georgia Dome didn't go as hoped. Atlanta's Matt Bryant kicked a 47-yard field goal with just nine seconds left, and the Falcons prevailed, 20–17. The loss was a major blow to the Packers' hopes of having homefield advantage throughout the postseason.

"It's discouraging not to win a game we should have won," Rodgers said.

Rodgers did all he could. Green Bay's running game was in hibernation again, so McCarthy put the offense in his quarterback's hands. Rodgers threw for 344 yards and led the Packers on a memorable 90-yard, game-tying drive in the final minute. On fourth-and-goal from the Atlanta 10, Rodgers fired a dart to Jordy Nelson that tied the game, 17–17.

"You go down and score a touchdown, and you're thinking overtime," said Rodgers, who also had a critical fumble at the goal line in the second quarter. "Tying the game was pretty special."

But after a 40-yard kick return by Atlanta's Eric Weems and a face-mask penalty on Green Bay's Matt Wilhelm, the Falcons needed to move just 20 yards for the winning kick.

Atlanta was now 9–2 and in control of the NFC race. The Packers had dropped to 7–4 and had fallen behind Chicago in the NFC North.

"I have no plans of going to Lambeau Field in January," Falcons wideout Roddy White said. "I plan on staying right here and sleeping in my own bed in the playoffs."

White would eventually get his wish. The Packers, meanwhile, again had work to do.

It started with an impressive 34–16 dismantling of San Francisco. The 49ers had passed on Rodgers at the top of the 2005 draft, and there was nothing he enjoyed better than making them pay. Rodgers did exactly that on this day, throwing three TD passes—including two to Greg Jennings—and for 298 total yards. Interestingly, the 49ers were still searching for a suitable quarterback. Alex Smith, the player San Francisco selected instead of Rodgers at No. 1, had fizzled. And the 49ers were now playing journeyman Troy Smith.

"I think every player, particularly quarterbacks, the path that you're put on has a lot to do with your success," McCarthy said when talking of Rodgers and Smith. "There's a lot of factors that go into developing a quarterback. Obviously they both had unique ability to even be considered to be part of the conversation of being the No. 1 pick in the National Football League."

This was the latest example, though, of how the 49ers would have given anything to have that pick back. Rodgers threw TD passes of 57 yards and 1 yard to Jennings. Driver also caught a 61-yard TD that will forever be part of the Packers' 2010 highlight reel.

On Green Bay's opening drive of the second half and the Packers facing a second-and-16 at their own 39, Driver lined up in the right slot. He found a hole in San Francisco's zone and hauled in a strike from Rodgers at the 49ers' 38. Driver spun away from safety Reggie Smith at the 30, then ducked under a tackle attempt by safety Dashon Goldson at the 22. Cornerback Nate Clements had an angle on Driver, but Driver simply shoved him out of the way at the 10.

Three 49ers finally corralled Driver at the 4, but he dragged them into the right corner of the end zone for an improbable 61-yard TD and a 21–13 Green Bay lead.

"Donald made one of the most amazing catches and runs I've ever seen," Rodgers said. "We nicknamed him 'The Kickstand.' That's been his nickname around here since I've been here. When he was at about the 20, I was thinking, 'Go down, go down, don't get drilled,' and then when he broke another tackle I was hoping he'd get it in the end zone."

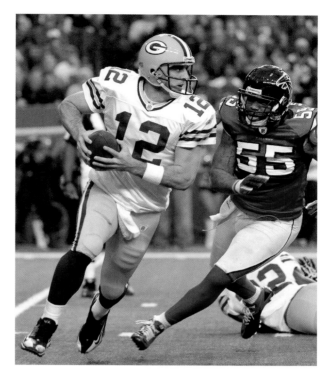

The game also marked the debut of rookie running back James Starks, who spent the first 12 weeks of the year either inactive or on the physically-unable-to-perform list. But Starks proved worth the wait, rushing for 73 yards on 18 carries in his season debut.

"I was just keeping my eyes open," Starks said. "Whatever was asked of me, I was ready for it. I prepared well in practice and was just ready for the opportunity."

With a quarter of the regular season remaining, the Packers also appeared ready to make their move. Instead, all of their best-laid plans were swept away the following week after a shocking 7–3 loss in Detroit. Rodgers was knocked out of the game in the second quarter with his second concussion of the year. Green Bay's offense had been brutal with Rodgers and also struggled with backup Matt Flynn.

And when Lions third-string quarterback Drew Stanton threw a fourth-quarter TD to tight end Will Heller, Detroit snapped a 19-game losing streak to their NFC North foes.

"I can't really measure the level of a concussion at this point," McCarthy said afterward in regard to

Aaron Rodgers scrambles away from Atlanta's John Abraham during a Week 12 showdown. The Falcons rallied late, though, to post a 20–17 win.

"We're nobody's underdog," McCarthy boldly proclaimed. "We have all the confidence in our abilities. We've had challenges throughout the season. We've stepped up to those challenges, and we feel the same way going into this game."

One will never know if that was false bravado or not. New England's last three wins had been by an average of 30.7 points. But the Packers certainly didn't play like anybody's underdog. Backup quarterback Matt Flynn played extremely well subbing for Rodgers and threw three TD passes. Flynn also drove the Packers to the Patriots' 15-yard line in the closing seconds, but he was sacked on the final play of the game.

Despite the defeat, the Packers left Foxboro that night fully believing in themselves once again. If they could go blow-for-blow with arguably football's best team—and do it without Rodgers—they could play with anybody, right?

"I think that was a huge point in our season for our confidence," Driver said. "We didn't win the game. But after that game, we knew we could play with anybody again."

On that same Sunday, the Packers caught an enormous break when Philadelphia's DeSean Jackson returned a punt 65 yards on the final play of the game to lift the Eagles past the New York Giants, 38–31. The Eagles (10–4) were likely headed to the playoffs regardless of that outcome. But with the Giants (9–5) losing and coming to Lambeau Field the following week, the Packers once again controlled their own postseason fate.

"Our playoffs started when we got on the plane to come home," McCarthy said. "That's the way we're approaching our preparation, that's the way we're approaching this game. It's going to be a playoff-type atmosphere here at home."

The key to everything, of course, was Rodgers. By Tuesday, Rodgers was cleared to play. He then proceeded to have one of the best games of his young life.

Rodgers threw for a career-high 404 yards, tied a personal best with four touchdown passes, and posted

Rodgers. "He'll go through the normal protocol this week. I was just told that his head is clear, and he has a headache."

Green Bay's season was undeniably at a crossroads. The Packers had now lost two of three and were on the outside looking in at the playoff race. Rodgers would miss Green Bay's next game in New England. And the Packers' final three opponents were a combined 29–10 (.744), giving Green Bay the toughest remaining schedule in football.

The first team on that murderer's row was mighty New England, winners of five straight and boasting an NFL-best 11–2 record. Although Green Bay entered the game a 14-point underdog, McCarthy wasn't treating this as a David vs. Goliath affair.

(above) Rodgers was aided by a rejuvenated running attack in leading Green Bay to a 34–16 trouncing of the 49ers in Week 13. (opposite) After missing a game and a half because of a concussion, Rodgers returned to form in spectacular fashion against the Giants. He passed for a career-high 404 yards in leading the Packers to a 45–17 victory.

the third-highest passer rating of his career (139.9). The result was a stunning 45–17 rout of the New York Giants that put the Packers back in control of their playoff destiny.

"It was fun," Rodgers said. "I had a good week of preparation this week. I think that's kind of where it started. I felt good throwing the ball all week, liked the game plan, liked the things we were trying to do, and once we were into the game, I liked the rhythm that Mike [McCarthy] had our offense in."

Rodgers switched to a new helmet that had additional padding. The goal was to lower the risk of another concussion, but because Rodgers' face was jammed into the helmet, he took a lot of grief from teammates. While Rodgers' face may have looked funny, there was nothing comical about his arm.

"I felt all week a lot of energy," Rodgers said. "My arm felt like it was live. I threw the ball really good in practice, so I had a lot of confidence going into the game that I was going to perform this way—obviously, not maybe as well as it went—but I think you can contribute that to some really good play calls at certain times and some big plays by some guys."

One of the few tense moments came late in the first quarter, when Rodgers took off running. As the Lambeau Field faithful held their collective breath, Rodgers picked up 15 yards and then slid before getting walloped. Rodgers proceeded to jump up and signal "safe." At that moment, the sellout crowd went berserk. It was only the start, as Rodgers shredded the Giants' secondary and put the Packers back on track for a playoff berth.

"We were ready to play," Jennings said. "We prepared all week with the focus and mind-set of this is it—this is our season. In front of this crowd and in our own backyard, we can't go down like that. We came out here and gave it our best shot, and it was a great shot today."

Only one test remained: the archrival Chicago Bears. While the Bears had already clinched the NFC North title and a first-round bye, they wanted nothing more than to knock their oldest rival out of the postseason. That's why Chicago coach Lovie Smith played his starters the entire way, even though theoretically, the Bears had nothing to gain with a win.

"We're playing to win the game," Smith insisted.

And Chicago did throughout the memorable 181st tussle between these teams. But Rodgers hit tight end Donald Lee with a 1-yard TD pass early in the fourth quarter to give the Packers a thrilling 10–3 win.

"It feels incredible," said Packers outside linebacker Erik Walden, who had a career day with $2\frac{1}{2}$ sacks and 16 tackles. "It didn't always look great for us, but we got it done."

The Packers got it done thanks to a terrific defensive effort that limited the Bears to 227 total yards and just 97 yards after halftime. Green Bay sacked Bears quarterback Jay Cutler six times, had two interceptions, and limited Cutler to a 43.5 passer rating—less than half his season average.

"I don't know if it was our best [defensive] game this year or not," Packers nose tackle B.J. Raji said. "But if it wasn't, it was close."

Green Bay's win gave it the sixth and final NFC playoff berth and knocked the New York Giants out of the postseason. The Packers, Giants, and Tampa Bay all finished with 10–6 records, but Green Bay won the tiebreaker based on strength of victory.

Afterward, the Packers were elated to have overcome an inordinate number of injuries to reach the postseason. As Chicago's bus rolled out of Lambeau Field that frigid night, many Bears had a different thought.

"I kept thinking we're going to see them again," Bears cornerback Tim Jennings said of the Packers. "I was thinking, 'Man, we should have knocked them out.'"

Jennings didn't know how right he was. ∎

After yet another must-win victory—this one 10–3 over the Bears—a relieved Aaron Rodgers trots off Lambeau Field en route to his second foray into the playoffs.

RETURN TO THE PLAYOFFS

Green Bay's postseason almost ended as quickly as it began. Thanks to Tramon Williams, the Packers' run to greatness was only getting started. The Packers had controlled play throughout much of their wild-card game in Philadelphia. They had been sharp on offense early, stout on defense throughout, and led the entire way. But late in the contest, the Eagles closed to within 21–16 and drove to Green Bay's 27-yard line.

On first-and-10, Eagles quarterback Michael Vick faked a throw down the middle and then threw for rookie Riley Cooper in the left corner of the end zone. Williams never bit on the ball fake, though, and had perfect position to intercept Vick's pass with 33 seconds left and send the Packers to the NFC Divisional Game.

"I feel like I got greedy and took a shot at the end zone," Vick said. "I didn't throw the ball I wanted and got picked. It's not the way I wanted to go out, but I went down swinging."

Aaron Rodgers was swinging throughout, as well, and became the first Packers quarterback other than Brett Favre to win a postseason game since Lynn Dickey on January 8, 1983. Rodgers threw three touchdowns, completed 66.7 percent of his 27 passes, and had a lights-out passer rating of 122.5.

Rodgers had been criticized in some circles throughout 2010 for never winning a playoff game. Of course, he'd only had one opportunity and helped the 2009 Packers score 45 points at Arizona.

"Well, in all my time being a football fan I have never seen one player win a game all by himself," Rodgers said. "It is a good team win for us, and I will let you guys write what you want on that."

Rodgers was huge as the Packers jumped on the Eagles early. He threw a seven-yard TD pass to tight end Tom Crabtree—the first of Crabtree's career—and a nine-yard score to James Jones as Green Bay jumped out to a 14–0 lead. After the Eagles closed to within 14–10 early in the third quarter, Rodgers threw a screen pass to running back Brandon Jackson that he took 16 yards for a TD.

"I'm probably biased, but I think Aaron Rodgers is probably as good an in-and-out-of-the-pocket quarterback as there is in football today," Packers coach Mike McCarthy said. "His ability to play in the pocket, trusting his footwork, the time clock, the ability to come out of the pocket to buy time, that's Aaron's strength.

"And on top of that...he has the arm strength to make all of the throws. It gives you a lot of versatility as a play-caller and as an offensive schemer when you have a quarterback right now with his experience, playing as well as he is. He's a special player."

To the surprise of the football world, Packers rookie running back James Starks was extremely special on this afternoon, as well. Starks, who had just 101 rushing yards during the regular season, erupted for 123 yards on 23 carries. Starks' total established a Packers

Aaron Rodgers had three touchdown passes and a 122.5 passer rating as the Packers defeated Philadelphia 21–16 in their NFC wild-card game.

"I'M PROBABLY BIASED, BUT I THINK AARON RODGERS IS PROBABLY AS GOOD AN IN-AND-OUT-OF-THE-POCKET QUARTERBACK AS THERE IS IN FOOTBALL TODAY. —Mike McCarthy

rookie postseason record, breaking the old mark of 88 yards held by Travis "The Roadrunner" Williams set in 1967. Starks' output was also the highest by a Green Bay running back in 2010, topping Brandon Jackson's 115-yard effort against Washington in Week 5.

"The way that James Starks was running the ball tonight was maybe one of the most important factors in this win," Rodgers said. "He ran great, and I am so happy for him. He is a great kid, and he has really grown a lot in the past couple weeks. He was big tonight."

In the end, though, it came down to Green Bay's defense. And thanks to Wiliams, the Packers were moving on.

"Tramon Williams has clearly played at a Pro Bowl level, there's no question about it," McCarthy said. "Tramon Williams, he has done it all year. He has been playing at this level all year."

Williams was just getting started. So was Rodgers.

Atlanta, the NFC's No. 1 seed with a 13–3 regular season record, was about to pay the price. The Falcons entered their NFC Divisional Playoff game against Green Bay with two full weeks of rest. The Falcons were extremely confident after defeating the Packers in their own building just two months earlier.

But on a memorable Saturday night for Packer Nation, the Rodgers-Williams duo was beyond dynamic and led Green Bay to a 48–21 destruction of the Falcons. Rodgers, making just his third postseason start, had a game for the ages in the Georgia Dome. He completed 31 of 36 passes for 366 yards, three touchdowns, no interceptions, and posted a passer rating of 136.8.

Williams had two interceptions in a two-and-a-half-minute window late in the first half. The first stopped a potential Falcons touchdown, then Williams went 70 yards with the second interception for a game-changing touchdown.

"To see your big-time players step up in the primetime games, that's what it's all about," Packers coach Mike McCarthy said.

The Packers were dominant on both sides of the ball throughout. But no one stepped up more than Rodgers or Williams. Rodgers' performance against Atlanta was arguably the greatest postseason game ever by a Packers quarterback and one of the finest in NFL history.

Rodgers set Packers playoff records for completions (31) and completion percentage (86.1 percent) and had the second-most postseason passing yardage in team history (366). In 10 possessions, Rodgers led Green Bay to five touchdowns, two field goals, and the Packers never punted.

"This probably was my best performance—the stage we were on, the importance of this game," Rodgers said afterward. "It was a good night."

Rodgers threw touchdown passes to Jordy Nelson (6 yards), James Jones (20), and John Kuhn (7). Rodgers was razor sharp, shredded what had been a respectable defense, and got plenty of help from his gifted wideouts. The most impressive part of Rodgers'

night, though, might have been his feet. On several plays, Atlanta standout defensive end John Abraham seemed ready to dump Rodgers. But the nifty quarterback escaped and even had a seven-yard TD run.

Williams, on the other hand, made a series of game-changing plays. And one week after notching the game-saving interception in Philadelphia, Williams was even better against the Falcons.

With the game tied at 14 late in the second quarter, Falcons quarterback Matt Ryan took a shot to the end zone for 6-foot-4 wideout Michael Jenkins. But the 5′11″ Williams played the ball better, and when Jenkins lost his footing, Williams went up and picked Ryan off with 2:20 left in the first half.

"I think we have lots of guys on the defense that can make those plays," Williams said. "I think I've just been put in that position the last couple of weeks and made those plays for my teammates. I don't see it as a big deal."

Oh, it was a big deal. And right before the half, Williams made a play that was an even bigger deal.

Green Bay had taken a 21–14 lead, but Atlanta was driving into field-goal range and had reached the Packers' 35. With just 10 seconds left in the half, Ryan rolled left and threw back across his body for Roddy White. Williams jumped the route, though, made a nifty cut past Ryan at midfield, and then sailed to the end zone to make it 28–14.

When the Packers scored on their first drive of the third quarter and increased their lead to 35–14, this one was essentially over.

"I think everything he's done, every good thing that's happened to Tramon on the field, all the plays he's making he deserves," Packers linebacker A.J. Hawk said of Williams. "I've never been around probably a better teammate than a guy like Tramon. He's awesome. I love how he prepares. He does everything right."

Against the Falcons, both Rodgers and Williams did virtually everything right. Now, it was on to Chicago with a Super Bowl berth at stake. Just three weeks earlier, the Bears had a chance to end Green

Rodgers scrambles around Falcons linebacker Curtis Lofton for a seven-yard touchdown run during the second half of the Packers' playoff rout of Atlanta.

Bay's season. Now, Chicago was wishing it had done exactly that.

Although the Bears had the homefield advantage, Green Bay was coming to Soldier Field as arguably football's hottest team. And even though the Packers finished second to Chicago in the NFC North and were going on the road, Green Bay was installed as a three-point favorite.

"It's going to be backyard football," said Bears defensive end Israel Idonije. "Man on man. They throw a punch, we throw a punch. We're going to slug back and forth, and the first one to flinch or drop is going to lose the game."

This would be the 182nd meeting in this storied rivalry. Amazingly, though, these bitter adversaries had played just once in the postseason. That came in 1941, when George Halas' Bears defeated Curly Lambeau's Packers 33–14 in a Western Division playoff game played at Wrigley Field in Chicago.

The two fan bases were in a frenzy beforehand. So were the teams.

"I think it takes the rivalry to the next level," Rodgers said. "It's great that there's so much history, the longest-running rivalry in the National Football League. To have one of us, the winner of this game, go to the Super Bowl is pretty special."

It was even more special when Rodgers and his teammates were presented the Halas Trophy following their 21–14 win over Chicago in the NFC Championship Game. Green Bay was far from perfect, failing to score an offensive point after taking a 14–0 lead early in the second quarter. But the Packers got a big day from their defense and notched the franchise's biggest win in 13 years.

"We would have liked to put more than 14 points on the board, obviously, but we're going to the Super Bowl," Rodgers said. "We've got a week to relax and get our bodies back and go enjoy Dallas and hopefully get a win down there."

The way the Packers started against the Bears, it looked like they'd breeze to Dallas.

On Green Bay's first drive, Rodgers led a seven-play, 84-yard march that he capped with a one-yard TD run. Rodgers was 4-for-4 on the march for 76 yards and hit Greg Jennings twice for 48 yards.

"Frankly, the first drive was the way we anticipated coming into this game," McCarthy said. "I thought we were able to get into a tremendous rhythm."

Green Bay stayed in rhythm and went ahead 14–0, just four minutes into the second quarter. The Packers needed only five plays to cover 44 yards on that drive. Running back Brandon Jackson (16 yards) and wideout Jordy Nelson (15) both had big catches on the march, and running back James Starks finished the deal with a four-yard TD run.

"The way we started out, I thought we were going to put up 40 points on [Chicago]," Packers right guard Josh Sitton said. "We came out and were running good, throwing good, just rolling like Atlanta."

Yes, for a little more than a quarter, this felt exactly like the NFC Divisional Playoffs, when the Packers drilled the Falcons 48–21. From that point forward, though, everything changed.

In Green Bay's first four possessions, it rolled up 181 total yards, had 12 first downs, and averaged 7.9 yards per play. In the Packers' final 10 possessions, they had 175 total yards, 11 first downs, and averaged just 3.9 yards per play.

"It was weird, man," Packers wideout James Jones said. "We don't feel like there's anybody out there that can stop us except us. And the rest of the game, I'd just say we stopped ourselves."

Fortunately for Green Bay, though, its defense stole the show. The Packers forced three turnovers, held Chicago's three quarterbacks to a combined passer rating of 45.2, and allowed just 132 total yards through three quarters. "It seems the defense has put these last three games away," linebacker Clay Matthews said. "We had our backs against the wall a little bit, but we made the play to win the game."

Leading the charge were undrafted rookie cornerback Sam Shields and second-year nose tackle B.J.

Raji. Shields had a pair of interceptions, including one with 37 seconds left and Chicago driving for the potential game-tying score. Raji also bailed out Green Bay's struggling offense with an 18-yard interception return for a touchdown midway through the fourth quarter.

"It's an unbelievable feeling," said Shields, who entered the game with two interceptions all year. "There's a lot of guys that wait a long, long time for this. Now, we're going to the Super Bowl."

Shields was a major reason why. Late in the first half the Bears trailed 14–0, but had seized momentum after Lance Briggs intercepted Rodgers. Two plays later, Chicago quarterback Jay Cutler took a shot down the left sideline for wideout Johnny Knox.

Shields, who played wideout for three years at the University of Miami, ran stride for stride with Knox, then turned and almost became the receiver. Shields had inside leverage, got to the ball before Knox, and made a gorgeous pick.

"I just got my head around and went to the highest point," said Shields, who also had a sack.

Shields' second interception was the biggest play he's made as a Packer.

Caleb Hanie, Chicago's third-string quarterback, had rallied the Bears to within 21–14 late in the fourth quarter. Chicago had driven to Green Bay's 29-yard line, had a fourth-and-5, and still had 47 seconds to notch the equalizer. Hanie worked out of the shotgun, the Bears sent out four receivers, and the Packers rushed five. Hanie took a shot down the middle for Knox, but Shields jumped the route knowing safety Nick Collins was providing help from behind.

Aaron Rodgers led the Packers on a seven-play, 84-yard touchdown march on their first possession of the NFC Championship Game. The Packers would never trail.

With his coaches screaming, 'Get down,' Shields returned the interception 32 yards. When Shields rose up, he was mobbed by teammates that knew their next stop was the Super Bowl.

"We need to work on that last play, getting on the ground a little sooner," Packers coach Mike McCarthy joked. "Sam, for a rookie—and I told a couple other rookies this—you have no idea what you've accomplished here in your first year in the league. He is going to be a great player for the Green Bay Packers for a long time."

Raji certainly fit that bill, as well. With the Packers clinging to a 14–7 lead midway through the fourth quarter, Raji made a play that McCarthy called a "game-winner." The Bears had a third-and-5 from their own 15. Raji lined up over center Olin Kreutz, showed blitz, and then dropped into the middle of the field where Hanie was trying to get the ball to running back Matt Forte.

Hanie never saw Raji and threw the ball right into his enormous mitts. Raji caught the ball naturally and then waltzed to the right corner of the end zone to make it 21–7. Raji didn't have an interception in the NFL or college, so his timing was ideal for Packer Nation.

"It's just a great feeling," Raji said. "It was a great call. I was behind the back, and obviously he wasn't expecting that. I just caught it and ran it back."

The play was one of the most memorable in Packers playoff history. And now, Green Bay was headed back to the Super Bowl for the first time since 1997, where it would face AFC giant Pittsburgh.

"I'm numb," said McCarthy, who grew up in Pittsburgh and was an assistant coach at the University of Pittsburgh from 1989 to 1992. "It's a great feeling. I'm just so proud of our football team. As I said, we have a goal of playing 16 quarters, and we've completed 12. We're fired up and getting ready to go to Dallas, Texas."

Getting ready for the time of their lives. ■

Aaron Rodgers didn't have any touchdown passes in the NFC Championship Game, but he did run for one score.

CHAMPIONS OF THE FOOTBALL WORLD

Experience. As Super Bowl XLV approached, *experience* was the buzzword. The Pittsburgh Steelers had tons of it. The Green Bay Packers had very little. Would it make a difference? "When we get into the game, then it's just the Super Bowl," Packers fullback John Kuhn insisted. "It's the Super Bowl and the event that nobody has really experienced. The game is still the game."

The Packers were hoping that was true, because the Steelers' roster was dotted with past Super Bowl standouts. From Ben Roethlisberger to James Harrison to Hines Ward, Pittsburgh entered the world's biggest sporting event with a "been there, done that" attitude. In all, Pittsburgh had 14 starters that won a Super Bowl championship. The Steelers also had 10 players with two rings and a total of 25 players that had competed in a Super Bowl.

Green Bay had not been to a Super Bowl since 1997. And the only Packers to ever play in a Super Bowl were cornerback Charles Woodson and defensive end Ryan Pickett, and both played on losing teams. Green Bay insisted, though, that once the ball was kicked, none of that would matter.

"I look at it like the hungry dog hunts harder than the fat dog," said Packers tight end Donald Lee. "And we have a lot of hungry dogs in this locker room that are willing to do whatever it takes to win that game. I'm sure they're willing to do what it takes, too, but if I were a betting man, I'd bet my money on the hungry dog."

This was Pittsburgh's third Super Bowl appearance in six years. The Steelers defeated Seattle and Arizona in the 40th and 43rd Super Bowls, respectively, and many of the key cogs from those teams still remained. Ward was the MVP of Super Bowl XL after catching five passes for 123 yards and a touchdown. Harrison had a 100-yard interception return for a touchdown in Super Bowl XLIII. And Roethlisberger was the winning quarterback in each of those games.

Others, like Pro Bowl safety Troy Polamalu, mammoth nose tackle Casey Hampton, steady tight end Heath Miller, and splendid linebackers LaMarr Woodley, James Farrior, and Larry Foote, all played a role in Pittsburgh's recent success. Even 38-year-old head coach Mike Tomlin, in his fourth year, had a Super Bowl win on his résumé.

"It's meaningful," Packers head coach Mike McCarthy admitted. "But we're aware of it and understand that we haven't been there before, and that's something we'll talk about and make sure expectations and responsibilities [are] clear for everybody."

Green Bay's Super Bowl experience was less impressive. Kuhn was on the Steelers' practice squad in 2005 and got a ring after Pittsburgh beat Seattle in Super Bowl XL. Kuhn never played in that game, though. Pickett was a rookie with St. Louis in 2001 when the Rams lost to

Aaron Rodgers and the Green Bay Packers couldn't match the championship-game experience of Pittsburgh entering Super Bowl XLV, but in the end, it didn't seem to matter.

New England in Super Bowl XXXVI. And Woodson was part of Oakland's 2002 team that was routed by Tampa Bay in Super Bowl XXXVII.

"I believe if we stay calm and stay cool and understand what's going on, everything will work out," Packers running back Brandon Jackson said. "We've been on the big stage before, not as big as this, but as far as playoffs and everything like that, we've been on that type of stage. We're going to handle our business, stay calm and cool, and everything will work out."

The Packers agreed that Pittsburgh's experience could be an advantage in the days leading up to the game. Super Bowl week is packed with potential distractions, and that experience was going to be new to most of Green Bay's players. But the Packers also believed that once kickoff arrived, it was just back to football.

"The biggest thing is...trying to manage your schedule and keep it as similar as you can to what it would be like in a normal week," Rodgers said. "There's going to be a bunch of different things pulling at you... There's going to be a lot of different things that could disrupt your week if you let them."

Green Bay's week was fantastically quiet, though, which is just what head coach Mike McCarthy and his staff hoped for. The Packers had a mini-controversy shortly before Super Bowl week on whether or not the 15 players on injured reserve would be included in the team picture. Eventually they were, and that issue was settled before Green Bay got to Dallas.

Roethlisberger actually made the most noise in the days leading up to the game. The Steelers' quarterback was seen at a karaoke bar in Fort Worth, Texas, belting out Billy Joel's "Piano Man" and several other songs on the Tuesday of Super Bowl week.

"Tuesday night I take my linemen out to dinner, and we went to a great barbeque spot," Roethlisberger said. "We went there and wanted to listen to some live music, so we went to a piano bar. We just had an enjoyable night."

Rodgers, on the other hand, did the exact opposite.

"I haven't been out carousing," he said. "I am a homebody so I've been spending a lot of time in my hotel room watching film. I think it is important at the same time that you are sticking with your normal routine. I like to go out to dinner when I'm back home in Green Bay so I've gone out to dinner, to a couple of really nice spots, and then come home, relax, and watch film."

In general, though, the week was largely anticlimactic. The Steelers changed hotels on Saturday to avoid distractions. The Packers stayed put. Green Bay held a chapel session Saturday at 8:30 PM and had a 9:00 PM team meeting. But when all of the speeches and pep talks had ended, McCarthy made perhaps his boldest decision of the 2010 season.

He told his team to go and get fitted for Super Bowl rings. Amazingly, McCarthy had that on the team's itinerary for Saturday night.

"I talked to our football team a lot about having real confidence, and those are just examples and opportunities to express that," said McCarthy, who was born and raised in Pittsburgh. "I felt that the measurement of the rings, the timing of it would be special, it would have a significant effect on our players doing it the night before the game.

"Scheduling is so important during the course of the week, and you want to do certain things at certain times, and I felt that was the appropriate time. I thought it would be special. I thought it would give us a boost of confidence to do it the night before the game."

When game day arrived, Green Bay's collective confidence couldn't have been higher. McCarthy built his offensive game plan around Rodgers, who had shredded these same Steelers just 14 months earlier. McCarthy loved the matchups of his receivers against Pittsburgh's secondary, and now it was up to Green Bay's line to protect and for Rodgers to deliver.

"A huge part of our game plan was really putting the ball in Aaron Rodgers' hands," McCarthy said.

Defensively, the emergence of Packers cornerbacks Tramon Williams and Sam Shields had Green Bay's

secondary in far better shape than 2009. The Steelers had also dealt standout receiver Santonio Holmes away the previous offseason and were thin behind starters Mike Wallace and Hines Ward.

Steelers running back Rashard Mendenhall had emerged as a force in his third season and would be a huge challenge for Green Bay's mediocre run defense. In the end, though, the Packers fully believed the game would be decided by one category.

"We have to not turn the ball over," Rodgers said. "This team thrives on forcing turnovers, and if we can hang on to the football and not turn it over we are going to have a good chance to win."

Less than 12 minutes into the game, the Packers' chances of victory had increased exponentially. On Green Bay's second possession of a scoreless game,

Rodgers went to work on the Steelers secondary. Sharp, accurate, rhythmic, Rodgers hooked up twice with wideout Jordy Nelson for 18 total yards and brilliantly avoided pressure to find Brandon Jackson for 14 yards.

The Packers had driven to the Steelers' 29-yard line, when on third-and-1, they lined up with two tight ends and Nelson the lone receiver split far right. Pittsburgh anticipated a run, and that left Nelson one-on-one with mediocre cornerback William Gay.

Gay came to the line to play press coverage, but Nelson beat him by faking inside and then releasing down the right sideline. The Packers' offensive line did their jobs, and then Rodgers lofted a perfect fade to the right corner of the end zone. Nelson had a step on Gay and won a hand-fighting battle between the two. Nelson then hauled in Rodgers' gorgeous toss to

Aaron Rodgers and the Packers were brimming with confidence throughout Super Bowl week.

"THIS TEAM THRIVES ON FORCING TURNOVERS, AND IF WE CAN HANG ON TO THE FOOTBALL AND NOT TURN IT OVER WE ARE GOING TO HAVE A GOOD CHANCE TO WIN. —Aaron Rodgers"

give the Packers a 7–0 lead with 3:44 left in the first quarter.

"It was just press (coverage)," Nelson said. "Aaron gave me a little signal if it was press to go deep. It was actually a screen play, but he checked to a go route. That's what we hit."

Green Bay's hitting had only begun.

Pittsburgh began its next drive on its own 7-yard line after an illegal block penalty. And on the first play, Roethlisberger made the game's biggest blunder. Green Bay rushed just four, but Roethlisberger was trying to hit a home run to Wallace so he needed substantial time for the play to develop. That allowed beefy defensive end Howard Green, who was signed off the street in October when the Packers were ravaged by injury, to get home.

Green whipped left guard Chris Kemoeatu and then drilled Roethlisberger as he let loose a bomb for Wallace. Green's pressure caused Roethlisberger's pass to be severely underthrown, and Packers safety Nick Collins intercepted. Collins, who has been named to three straight Pro Bowls, took off down the right sideline and made a nifty cut back inside. When Collins reached the 3-yard line, he jumped and reached the end zone.

In a matter of 24 seconds, Green Bay had surged to a 14–0 lead.

"Oh man, that was the highlight of my day right there," Collins said. "I was able to read Big Ben [Roethlisberger] and got a nice jump on the ball. I made a couple cuts to get into the end zone."

Rodgers had stressed all week that turnovers would determine a winner. And late in the first half, he was beginning to look prophetic.

With the Packers leading 14–3, Pittsburgh was on the move. Operating out of the shotgun, Roethlisberger threw a short pass over the middle for Wallace, but cornerback Jarrett Bush read the crossing route, drove on the ball, and picked it off. Bush, one of the more maligned players in recent Packers history, developed into a special teams stalwart in 2010. But this was undoubtedly the biggest play he made from scrimmage during his five years in Green Bay.

"You know what, you've got to give them a lot of credit," Roethlisberger said. "They're a great defense. They got after us, and I turned the ball over, and you can't do that."

Especially with a quarterback like Rodgers on the other side.

Green Bay started on its own 47, and on its second play, Rodgers hit Nelson for 16 yards against nickel corner Bryant McFadden. Two plays later, Rodgers made one of his finest throws as a Packer. On a first-and-10 from Pittsburgh's 21, the Packers lined up four wide receivers. The Steelers rushed four and dropped seven. Greg Jennings lined up in the left slot and ran a deep seam route.

Jennings had gotten behind linebacker James Farrior and in front of safety Ryan Clark, but Rodgers' window was small, and his pass had to be perfect. It was. Rodgers delivered a dart that Clark missed by inches. Jennings took a wicked shot from safety Troy Polamalu, but he was already in the end zone.

The Packers led 21–3, with just more than two minutes remaining in the first half. Things couldn't be going any better.

"It was like they were a hair faster than we were all night," Clark said. Shortly before halftime, though, the Steelers were given new life.

At the two-minute mark, Shields left with a shoulder injury. Shields would return, but not until the fourth quarter. One play later, cornerback Charles Woodson—Green Bay's best free agent since Reggie White—suffered a broken collarbone and wouldn't return. Earlier in that second quarter, wideout Donald Driver left with an ankle injury and he wouldn't be back, either.

With the Packers shorthanded and scrambling defensively on that final series of the first half, Pittsburgh took full advantage. Roethlisberger threw for all 77 yards of the drive—highlighted by an eight-yard TD to Ward—and the Steelers pulled to within 21–10 just 39 seconds before halftime.

During the 30-minute intermission, an emotionally distraught Woodson tried addressing his teammates. "I was pretty emotional so I didn't get a whole lot out," Woodson said. "But just to tell them to get it done."

His message was heard.

"He could barely say much, he was very emotional and choked up," safety Charlie Peprah said of Woodson. "He got about three words out. He just said, 'You know how bad I want this,' and we knew what we had to do."

It certainly wasn't easy, though.

With Woodson and Shields sidelined, Green Bay was searching for defensive answers. But the Packers didn't have any early in the third quarter. After the Packers went three-and-out to start the half—a series that included a drop from James Jones that might have gone for a touchdown—Pittsburgh took over at midfield. Five running plays later, the Steelers had gone 50 yards, and Mendenhall was in the end zone.

Green Bay's lead, once as many as 18 points, had been whittled to 21–17. "It was tough," Packers defensive coordinator Dom Capers said. "We were scrambling there for a while, because a big part of our game plan went out the window. We planned on playing a lot of man coverage, and when those guys went out, we had to become more of a zone team."

Green Bay's struggles continued. One series after Jones had a critical drop, Nelson had a drop of his own—one of his three on the day—leading to a Packers punt. Green Bay's defense got a much-needed stop, but two offensive series later, Packers No. 5 wideout Brett Swain had a brutal drop. McCarthy challenged the play—and lost—and the Packers punted from deep in their territory.

"I'd say the whole game was a little bit different, not a lot of flow to it," Rodgers said. "After the pick six, we were on the sidelines for a long time in the first half. Never really got our momentum back until the fourth quarter on those last few drives. In a game like this with the long TV timeouts, you lose your sweat. You lose your feel."

The Packers had clearly lost their feel. And with the fourth quarter set to start, Pittsburgh had reached the Packers' 33-yard line trailing by just four points. On the first play of the quarter, though, Packers defensive end Ryan Pickett and linebacker Clay Matthews combined to blow up Mendenhall. Matthews stood him up on the front side, while Pickett got his helmet on the ball from behind and forced a fumble that linebacker Desmond Bishop recovered.

The Packers were back in business at Pittsburgh's 45-yard line, and Rodgers wasn't going to waste this golden opportunity. He proceeded to make three huge throws that gave Green Bay some comfort again. The first came on a third-and-7, when Rodgers rolled right and away from trouble. Jones ran a comeback route, and Rodgers drilled him for a 12-yard gain to keep the drive alive.

Then, after Nelson dropped a crossing route for a certain first down, the Packers faced a third-and-10 from Pittsburgh's 40. The Steelers rushed five, but couldn't get close to Rodgers, in large part because running back Brandon Jackson stoned McFadden in the hole. Nelson had single coverage and whipped Clark on an inside slant. The terrific blocking up front allowed Rodgers to step into the throw, and he delivered a strike to Nelson that went for 38 yards to Pittsburgh's 2-yard line.

"If you play this game long enough in this position, you are going to drop the ball," Nelson said. "You have to move on. We are level-headed. We don't get too high and we don't get too low as a whole wide receiver core. We weren't panicking at all when Pittsburgh started coming back. We just said, okay we have to go make plays. We knew it was going to be on us, and that is why we stepped up and made plays."

Rodgers and Jennings combined to make Green Bay's next big play. After Rodgers took a sack, the Packers had second-and-goal from Pittsburgh's 8-yard line. Green Bay employed an empty backfield, and after the ball was snapped, Rodgers quickly looked left.

Rodgers had no intention of ever going left, mind you. He was simply trying to get Polamalu—the NFL's Defensive Player of the Year—to drift that way. It was a continuation of a 60-minute battle that Rodgers waged—and won—with Polamalu.

"He's a guy that you have to be aware of him, where he's at all times," Rodgers said of Polamalu. "He's a great player, had a great season, but guys have to respect where my eyes are looking so it was important to me to use good eye control on the field and not stare anybody down because he can cover a lot of ground quickly.

"When he was down in the box, we made sure he was picked up in the protection schemes. A couple of times when he came on blitzes, we adjusted the protection to make sure we had him picked up because he's a very talented blitzer, and when he's high, a deep safety, you just have to make sure you are good with your eyes."

Rodgers was sublime on this play. Polamalu watched Rodgers' eyes and cheated back to the left, which allowed Jennings to come free in the right corner. Rodgers lofted another perfect ball, and Jennings' TD grab gave Green Bay a 28–17 lead.

"That was completely my fault," Polamalu said afterward. "Earlier in the game they ran Jennings down the middle, and I was anticipating that same pass play and I guessed wrong."

Pittsburgh answered right back, though, as Roethlisberger engineered a 66-yard TD drive that took just seven plays and slightly more than four minutes. The Steelers' scoring strike came when Wallace got behind Shields, and Roethlisberger put the ball right on his fingertips for a 25-yard touchdown.

Antwaan Randle El scored on an option pitch for the two-point conversion, and the Steelers were within 28–25. There was still 7:34 left in what had become a Super Bowl thriller.

"I thought we were going to win," Wallace said. "We never think we are going to lose. We have no doubt in our mind that we are going to win the game."

Rodgers and the Packers took over on their own 25, but after a sack and a false-start penalty on Daryn Colledge, they quickly faced a third-and-10. Pittsburgh rushed just three, which meant Rodgers would have to be razor sharp to beat the eight-man coverage in back. Jennings, working from the left slot, ran another seam route against Steelers No. 1 cornerback Ike Taylor. The ball was out of Rodgers' hands in 2.8 seconds, and he had perhaps a 12-inch window to squeeze the ball into.

He did. It was arguably the throw of Rodgers' life, one that went for 31 yards and kept the Steelers' offense on the sideline.

"It seemed like it brushed off the tip of Ike Taylor's glove," Jennings said. "But it just got over the top enough where I could make a play on it."

A pair of runs by James Starks netted 15 yards. Rodgers then threw a gorgeous back shoulder pass to Jones for 21 yards to Pittsburgh's 8-yard line. On third-and-goal, though, Rodgers' fade for Nelson in the right corner of the end zone missed by inches. Green Bay was forced to settle for a Mason Crosby field goal, and its lead was a precarious 31–25 with 2:07 still remaining.

"I was just disappointed we didn't finish off with seven," Rodgers said. "We talked about it with seven

Aaron Rodgers looks for a target downfield in the second half of Super Bowl XLV.

minutes left when we got the ball. 'Hey, let's take it down and score, and we're the champs.' We made a couple of big plays on third down, but unfortunately, I just missed Jordy (Nelson) on that third down on the goal line. I was just praying our guys would come up with one more stop."

Two years earlier, Roethlisberger led the Steelers 78 yards in the closing moments of Super Bowl XLIII and hit Holmes with a six-yard TD pass to win the game. Then in 2009, Roethlisberger and Wallace hooked up on a 19-yard TD on the final play of the game to defeat Green Bay 37–36. Now, Roethlisberger would get a chance to repeat history.

"We've been doing this all year long," said Tramon Williams, Green Bay's magnificent cornerback. "The defense has been put in that situation and that spot all year long, and we rose to the challenge each and every time. That's one thing we emphasized all season; that when adversity hits, that's when we want to step up and make plays, and we did that all year long."

Never more so than in the final two minutes. Pittsburgh began from its own 13 after a special teams penalty, but two Roethlisberger completions quickly took the ball to the 33. The Steelers seemed to have communication issues, though, and Roethlisberger threw consecutive incompletions to Wallace and Ward on balls that weren't even close. Now it was fourth-and-5, and Super Bowl XLV came down to one play. For the Packers, it was simple: make a stop and win a title.

"Everybody was just praying," Shields said.

Green Bay rushed five and ran a fire zone in back. Roethlisberger threw to his left for Wallace, but Williams broke on the ball perfectly and knocked it to the ground. The Steelers wanted a pass interference call, but Williams' technique was perfect, and no flags were warranted. Green Bay had held. Only 49 seconds remained.

"It was a great feeling because you knew that you had to go in and keep them from scoring a touchdown in the two-minute drill," Capers said. "A year ago when we played them up there, we had the same situation,

Wide receiver Greg Jennings and Aaron Rodgers hooked up for two touchdowns in the Super Bowl.

and they scored on the last play of the game to beat us. So it was a great feeling to see the play get made. That's the best feeling in the world."

There was one better: the kneel down. With Kuhn and Jackson huddled close, Rodgers took consecutive snaps and dropped to a knee. As the final seconds ticked off, Rodgers kept the ball in his hands, and that certainly seemed appropriate. Of all the reasons Green Bay had won its fourth Super Bowl and 13th NFL championship, Rodgers topped the list.

Rodgers was as crisp as a quarterback could be, and his 304 passing yards might have been 450 if it wasn't for the drops. His passer rating of 111.5 was the fourth-highest in Super Bowl history. Most importantly, though, Rodgers was terrific in taking care of the ball. He threw three TD passes, didn't have an interception or fumble, and was an easy choice for MVP.

"He made plays," Steelers coach Mike Tomlin said of Rodgers. "We didn't get turnovers. We know that they're capable of getting plays in chunks. We knew that they would throw the football quite a bit, and they did. He didn't fold under the pressure. I thought we hit him some early, we got to him as the game went on. But he showed his metal and continued to stand in there and throw the football and throw it accurately. I tip my hat to him for that."

So did Rodgers' teammates and coaches.

"To be honest, I didn't expect anything less from A-Rod," Packers nose tackle B.J. Raji said. "He's been doing this the whole season throughout the playoffs. He's emerged as our leader, and I believe the best is yet to come for him."

McCarthy couldn't have agreed more.

"He played great," McCarthy said. "We put everything on his shoulders. He did a lot at the line of scrimmage for us against a great defense. He did a hell of a job."

Truthfully, so did the entire 2010 Packers.

Left for dead when injuries struck, counted out when they were 8–6, the Packers never folded. And that resiliency, toughness, and heart led to an improbable six-game winning streak and a Super Bowl title to finish the season.

"The Super Bowl was the way our whole season was in one win," Bishop said. "Ups, downs, roller coaster rides, people getting hurt, and a momentum swing. We showed resilience again. We just kept fighting and stayed as one."

Added Woodson, "We just continued to get better all season. We continued to fight no matter what adversity we went through. I think late in the season, down the stretch, we just had fun, and today was no different, and world champs."

World champs is right.

The Vince Lombardi Trophy was headed back to Green Bay. Rodgers was able to don his title belt. And Green Bay's fans chanted 'Go Pack Go' while basking in the glow of another championship.

"The character in that locker room is like nothing I've ever been a part of," Rodgers said. "It's just a special group of guys who believe in each other and love each other. When someone goes down, somebody steps up and picks each other up."

That had been the case again on this glorious night. Rodgers and the Packers were champions of the football world. ■

Aaron Rodgers was giddy after leading the Packers past the Steelers in Super Bowl XLV.

2011: HISTORY AND HEARTBREAK

As the 2011 season arrived, Rodgers was still just 27 years old and in the prime of his life. He had just completed a remarkable season in which he was the Super Bowl MVP, was sensational throughout the postseason, and was playing with arguably the NFL's best roster.

Brett Favre was in a similar situation 14 years earlier and never won another championship. Now, the challenge for Rodgers was to collect another ring.

"Like Mike [McCarthy] always says, you've got to be good at handling success and understand that we're viewed differently now because we have won the championship," Rodgers said. "We need to be the hunter in this situation because we're going to be hunted."

Rodgers was certainly being viewed differently than a year or two earlier.

Rodgers overcame two concussions during the 2010 regular season, threw 28 touchdowns, and finished third in passer rating (101.2) and second in yards per attempt (8.3). But his playoff performance was an all-timer.

Rodgers threw nine postseason touchdown passes, which tied an NFL record. He also posted a 109.8 passer rating in the playoffs and was brilliant against both Atlanta (136.8) and Pittsburgh (111.5).

Rodgers was now widely viewed as football's third-best quarterback, behind only surefire Hall of Famers Tom Brady and Peyton Manning. With another ring, Rodgers could take another leap.

"I haven't really changed any of my offseason preparation or the things I like to do in the offseason," he said. "My challenge is from a physical standpoint—I've looked for new ways to challenge myself this offseason. I really focused on my diet and the way I eat—trying to get into peak shape, but also recognizing how your diet and food affects your energy levels and how your body reacts to stress and being on the field and the physical exertion you have to do."

Rodgers was in the best shape of his life. His mental and physical skills had both hit new heights. And Rodgers embarked on the season of a lifetime.

Rodgers and the Packers rolled through their early slate and hit the bye week 7–0. Green Bay won its first seven games by an average of 12.7 points and was scoring points like this was the Arena Football League.

The Packers averaged 32.9 points in their first seven games and eclipsed the 40-point plateau twice. And at this point in the season, Rodgers seemed a virtual shoo-in for league MVP honors.

Through seven games, Rodgers had a passer rating of 125.7, which was on pace to break Peyton Manning's single-season mark of 121.1 set in 2004. Rodgers had connected on 71.55 percent of his passes, which was ahead of Drew Brees' single-season mark of 70.62 set in 2009.

As Green Bay hit the bye week a perfect 7–0, Rodgers led the NFL with 20 touchdown passes. In addition, Rodgers was averaging an NFL-best 9.92

Aaron Rodgers winds up to pass during the Packers' 45–7 win over the Minnesota Vikings at Lambeau Field. In Green Bay's 15–1 regular season, Rodgers set franchise marks for TD passes (45) and passing yards (4,643), and established a new NFL record for passer rating (122.5), on the way to winning his first MVP award.

yards per passing attempt and had thrown just three interceptions.

"[Rodgers] is clearly the best decision maker that I've been around probably since my time in Kansas City with Joe Montana," McCarthy said. "[Rodgers] does not get bored throwing an easy completion, and that's a great attribute to have as a quarterback. He's clearly in tune taking what the defense gives you. He can throw the tight spots. He has the anticipation and arm strength and accuracy to attack the seams, but he does a great job of staying disciplined and staying within the offense."

His teammates certainly weren't arguing.

"There ain't nobody better right now," wideout James Jones said. "I'm not sure if there's ever been anybody better here. I'm not saying he's better than Brett, but Aaron's my quarterback and I'm always going to have his back. And I'm saying I'd take him over anybody because I got his back like that. He's my quarterback, and I'll take him over anybody that's playing today, yesterday, or in the future."

As the season marched on, it was amazing to see Rodgers and the Packers' offense continue to improve. Green Bay came out of its bye week and scored 45 points against both San Diego and Minnesota. The Packers hung 46 points on Oakland.

And as Green Bay headed to Kansas City in Week 15, it was a perfect 13–0.

"It's all about Kansas City," McCarthy said. "This is the target. This is the next mile marker. Our goal is homefield advantage all the way through to make sure we're playing playoff games in Lambeau Field. I know that's where my mind's at."

Unfortunately for Rodgers and the Packers, Kansas City is where the fun ended.

Green Bay's last loss had come in Week 15 in 2010, when the Rodgers-less Packers fell at New England. In the time since, Green Bay had rattled off a mind-boggling 19 consecutive wins.

But Kansas City ended the Packers' bid for a perfect 2011 campaign with a 19–14 win.

"It still sucks," Rodgers said of losing. "It's still not a fun feeling."

Amazingly, Green Bay's 19-game winning streak lasted a remarkable 357 days. From December 26, 2010, until December 18, 2011, the Packers didn't lose a game. And in today's world of parity, that's something that might not be seen again for several years.

"It's a pretty cool accomplishment to not lose in a year," Packers right tackle Bryan Bulaga said. "It is pretty cool. I've never been part of something where you win that many games in a row. Not many guys have."

"The Streak" contained a franchise-best 13–0 record to start the 2011 season and included 10 straight road wins.

It went down as the second-longest winning streak in NFL history, behind only the 2003–2004 New England Patriots (21). Most importantly, though, the Streak included a win over Pittsburgh in Super Bowl XLV.

"I've told so many people that this is something special," said wide receiver Donald Driver, who was completing his 13th season with Green Bay. "That streak—and what we have a chance to do this year—is something I think the fans will cherish for a long time. And not just the fans, the players too. We'll always cherish it."

Late in the 2010 season, Green Bay was 8–5 when it headed to New England without Rodgers (concussion). The Packers had just lost in Detroit, 7–3, were a double-digit underdog to the Patriots, and appeared to be in deep trouble.

Before that game, though, McCarthy declared, "We're nobody's underdogs," a message that seemed to revitalize his team.

The Packers lost four days later in New England, 31–27. But Green Bay thoroughly outplayed the Patriots that night, and many Packers left Foxboro, Massachusetts, with a renewed sense of hope.

"I think that New England game was definitely a turning point," guard Josh Sitton said. "Obviously our goal is to go out and win every game, but we went and

"THAT STREAK...IS SOMETHING I THINK THE FANS WILL CHERISH FOR A LONG TIME.

—Donald Driver

proved to them we can go frickin' play with anybody. I definitely think that was a turning point."

Rodgers returned the following week and threw four touchdowns in a 45–17 rout of the New York Giants. That win not only put the Packers in control of their own destiny, it gave them an enormous jolt of confidence.

"I think you have to go back to the first win when you talk about what got this thing rolling," Wells said of the Streak. "We had our backs against the wall that night, and came out and answered a lot of questions. We stepped up and peaked at the right time. Now, we've ridden that success into this season and have established our own success."

The Streak was packed with impressive achievements.

Green Bay didn't trail a single time in the fourth quarter of those 19 games. And only twice—against Chicago in Week 17 of 2010 and vs. the New York Giants in Week 13 of 2011—were the Packers tied in the fourth quarter.

Green Bay averaged 33.79 points per game during the Streak. And in seven of the 19 games, the Packers eclipsed 40 points.

Green Bay was plus-31 in takeaways during the Streak. And in the 19 games, Green Bay won the turnover battle 14 times, lost just once, and tied four others.

An NFL lockout that took away offseason practices didn't hurt Green Bay or lead to any complacency. Instead, when the Packers came back in 2011, they were focused on building what they started the previous season.

"I think at the beginning of this season we were so focused and everybody was buckled in like, 'Let's do it.' And that mindset and mentality has really helped us," safety Charlie Peprah said. "None of us got complacent. The mindset at the start of the year was, we're not defending anything. We're hunting. And I think that mindset really took hold in the locker room."

The Chiefs ended Green Bay's bid to become the first undefeated team since the 1972 Miami Dolphins. But the Packers viewed the setback as nothing more than a hiccup.

"I personally always viewed the undefeated season as really just gravy," McCarthy said. "The goal is to get the home-field advantage and win the Super Bowl."

Green Bay locked up homefield advantage for the first time in the Rodgers era with a 35–21 win over Chicago the following week. And Rodgers later won MVP honors after one of the best seasons in team history.

Rodgers set the franchise record for touchdown passes (45) and passing yards (4,643), and established a new NFL record for passer rating (122.5). On top of that, Rodgers had just six interceptions, completed 68.3 percent of his passes, led the NFL in yards per passing attempt (9.2), and led the Packers' offense to the second-most points (560) in NFL history at the time.

"Every Monday, when you watched the game from Sunday, you'd see the things that he did and how accurate he was and how productive he was," said Packers quarterbacks coach Tom Clements. "Just all along you knew he was having a great year."

Unfortunately for Rodgers and the Packers, that great year came to a screeching halt in the postseason.

Everything had gone right for Green Bay during a memorable 15–1 regular season. The offense scored a franchise record 560 points (a per-game average of 35).

Rodgers was sensational from start to finish. And Green Bay entered the playoffs as heavy favorites to become the first team since Denver in 1997–1998 to win consecutive Super Bowls.

But as the Packers readied for the NFC Divisional Playoff Game against the New York Giants, they were drilled with a sucker punch. Michael Philbin, the 21-year-old son of Packers offensive coordinator Joe Philbin, drowned early in week.

"A punch in the heart," McCarthy called Michael Philbin's death.

Joe Philbin, the father of six, was one of the most popular people in the Packers' organization. Philbin was a devoted family man who spoke often of his wife, Diane, and their children.

Philbin didn't call the plays on gamedays. That was McCarthy's baby. But Philbin had a huge role in game-planning during the week, was heavily involved in coaching the offensive line, and on game days, served as McCarthy's eyes and ears from the press box.

Philbin was certainly a grinder, someone who paid terrific attention to detail and was known as one of the staff's finest teachers. But Philbin also maintained levity with his dry wit and pleasant demeanor. So when Philbin lost his son, it was almost as if the entire organization lost a family member, too.

"Just a sad, sad time," Packers left guard T.J. Lang said. "Probably won't find a nicer guy on this staff than Joe. For that to happen to anybody is tragic, but to happen to a great guy like Joe makes it hurt that much more."

There's no way to ever know how much the crazy week affected the Packers during their playoff game with the Giants. But Green Bay played undoubtedly its poorest game of the season and suffered a 37–20 loss that ended an otherwise memorable campaign.

New York also defeated Green Bay in the 2007 NFC Championship Game at Lambeau Field. And in both instances, the Giants went on to win the Super Bowl.

"We got beat by a team that played better tonight," Rodgers said afterward. "That's the reality of this league. Been in for a while and been in the playoffs four times, and three times you lose your last game and you go home, and the one time you have that euphoric feeling that you keep fighting for. It's tough. Didn't think it was going to end tonight, felt good about our chances, felt good about our team. Personally, I didn't play as well as I wanted to."

Rodgers had been so good for the past year-and-a-half that he was almost taken for granted these days. Against the Giants, though, Packer Nation witnessed the type of mediocre quarterbacking that much of the league lives with each week.

Rodgers completed 56.5 percent of his 46 passes and his passer rating of 78.5 was his lowest in a full game since October 31, 2010. The Giants played mostly man coverage with two deep safeties, and when Rodgers refused to take chances, New York's pass rushers sacked him four times.

The most damaging sack came with 13 minutes left in the game, when Packers coach Mike McCarthy made the curious decision to go for it on fourth-and-5 from the Giants' 39-yard line. The Packers trailed just 20–13 at the time.

The Giants rushed five, while Green Bay protected with six and sent four pass catchers out in the pattern. Giants linebacker Michael Boley, the extra rusher, came off the right edge and got a clean release when tackle Bryan Bulaga blocked down.

That left Boley one-on-one with running back Brandon Saine. Boley looped all the way around Saine, came back to the inside, and dropped Rodgers from behind.

The play took 3.9 seconds, plenty of time for Rodgers to choose one of his targets. Instead, he ate the ball and left his team with no chance to convert the first down.

Ten plays later, the Giants had a 23–13 lead and the Packers were finished.

"Did we rattle him? Maybe a little bit," said Giants cornerback Aaron Ross, whose team lost to the Packers 38–35 on December 4. "I just think we did a good job

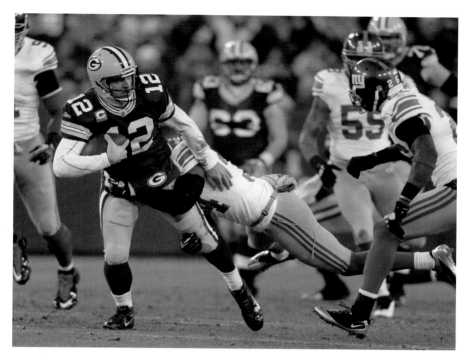

locking onto the receivers and taking away some places he wanted to go."

Even when Rodgers had clean looks, he made some throws that were uncharacteristic. One play before that fateful sack, Rodgers had Jermichael Finley wide open for a 15-yard gain on third-and-5. But Rodgers' led Finley too far, and when the tight end fully extended, the ball went off his fingertips.

"It was just, it was out in front of me. It was far out in front of me," Finley said. "As you saw, I put one hand out, tried to get it, but I've got to catch the ball."

Afterward, Rodgers was extremely animated, yelling at no one in particular about the play. It appeared, though, that Finley ran hard through his route and Rodgers simply missed him.

"I missed my spot maybe a little bit," Rodgers said. "But I'll have to go back and look at the film and see what happened."

Unofficially, the Packers had eight drops in the game, which made it tough for Rodgers to get in sync. Green Bay also had four turnovers, its most since October 3, 2010—a span of 32 games.

But the erratic quarterbacking play had to be the biggest shock in a stunning defeat.

"We all didn't play our best game," Rodgers said. "Personally, I didn't play as well as I...I did have a good week of practice, I felt like I was prepared, and I missed a couple of throws."

There wasn't much Rodgers missed during a memorable 2011 season. But the painful ending certainly left a rotten taste in everyone's mouths.

"No one's going to remember the 15–1," Packers nose tackle B.J. Raji said. "Now, all they're going to talk about is the great letdown at home, in front of your home fans that love you and support you."

Green Bay certainly wasn't the first team to have a historic regular season, then fall on its face in the postseason. Of the six teams to go 15–1 or better, only San Francisco (1984) and Chicago (1985) won the Super Bowl. Minnesota (1998) and Pittsburgh (2004) lost in the conference championship game, and New England (2007) lost in Super Bowl XLII.

The 2011 Packers, though, will now be remembered as the only 15–1 team that didn't win at least one playoff game. And that had everyone rather ornery.

"It's disappointing," Rodgers said. "We play to win championships. You win a championship and you're kind of at the top of the mountain, and you forget kind of how bad this feeling is. Had it after the 2009 season when we lost to Arizona, and it sucks. This team, this organization, this fan base expects championships. We had a championship-caliber regular season and didn't play well today." ■

Aaron Rodgers is brought down by Giants safety Deon Grant during the Packers' 37–20 playoff loss to New York in Green Bay.

2012: FALLING SHORT OF THE GOAL

Brett Goode has watched episodes of *Jeopardy* with Aaron Rodgers. And Goode, the Green Bay Packers' long snapper, always leaves rather amazed by the quarterback. "The guy's just smart across the board," Goode said of Rodgers. "His memory is incredible."

Jeff Saturday, Green Bay's starting center in 2012, noticed the same thing immediately after arriving in Green Bay. And Saturday had one overriding thought. "Aaron's memory is a lot like Peyton Manning's," said Saturday, who spent 12 seasons in Indianapolis snapping the ball to Manning. "We'd be in center-quarterback meetings early in the week, and he'd bring up some blitz that happened against Miami, or whatever, something that's pertinent to this week. He'd say, 'Oh, we got them on this blitz.' He just has a great recall for remembering those plays, and he'll adapt and adjust and look for ways to take advantage of that."

Rodgers' physical gifts—the big arm, terrific accuracy, and underrated athleticism—have been well-chronicled. But a Rain Man–like memory might be the most important of Rodgers' talents.

Once Rodgers sees a defense, he locks away all of its strengths, weaknesses, and tendencies. Rodgers studies the pros and cons of players throughout the league and can recite them in the blink of an eye. And while defensive coordinators might bounce from job to job, Rodgers never forgets how they like to attack.

As much as anything, it's Rodgers' mental skills that helped him win a Super Bowl in 2010 and NFL MVP honors in 2011.

"The ability to recall things quickly certainly helps," Rodgers said. "Of the most important things a quarterback can have, I think mental and physical toughness are at the top. Then a good memory is right near, kind of a near second tier. You have to be able to learn from your mistakes, but also recall information you saw during the week or from previous weeks or previous years very quickly. What that means to me is, when I'm visualizing things, you want to have a feeling after that visualization, a positive feeling or kind of a negative memory and kind of tag it in your brain that way. Then when it pops up again, it immediately hits your brain a certain way. Breaking the huddle and thinking about this play, I immediately recall either a positive or negative feeling from the memory I have associated with that—and being able to have a quick recall is important."

Rodgers noticed at a young age that certain things stuck in his head that seemed to escape many others. Especially with sports. Rodgers loved to play the old Strat-O-Matic baseball game. And to this day, he can still recite statistics from former San Francisco Giants players—which was his team of choice. In casual conversation, Rodgers points out that one-time Giants third baseman Kevin Mitchell had 47 home runs and 125 RBIs in 1989. Interestingly, he's exactly right.

Aaron Rodgers drops back to pass in the first half of a controversial loss to the Seahawks on *Monday Night Football* in Seattle.

Rodgers does the same with heroes from his youth like 49ers quarterback Joe Montana. "The more times you punch 'em on a calculator, the more times they become kind of stuck in your brain, what those averages and those ERAs are," Rodgers said. "I just liked doing quick math like that."

Rodgers certainly studied hard. But he admits learning came relatively easy, and once something was on the board, it was probably embedded in Rodgers' head. "He's just really damn smart...and he definitely knows how smart he is," Packers guard Josh Sitton said of Rodgers. "But to be a quarterback in this system, you have to be. He'll talk about a certain play or a certain defense, and he'll say something like, 'Oh, yeah. That was like the Bears did to us in '09.' The guy has a great memory."

Rodgers skipped a grade in math. He was in a gifted and talented program. Rodgers had straight As his first three semesters of high school. And the only C Rodgers had in high school came in calculus.

"I loved math, as long as it wasn't calculus," Rodgers jokes.

Rodgers loves to crunch numbers in his head or recite odd statistics. That quick mind and recall ability was a big reason Rodgers had a 3.6 GPA in college and a Wonderlic score of 35.

"I like the mental math," Rodgers said. "Just seeing things quickly can really help."

Especially on the football field.

Rodgers has copious notes from every game he's ever played. He'll review them each time he's set to face an opponent. But many of Rodgers' best notes are the ones deeply embedded in his brain.

"You can be sitting there talking to him and he can go back and remember exactly what happened on a certain play or at different times in games," said Goode, one of Rodgers' best friends. "This game has a lot of mental elements to it. And when you can recall other games and other situations, that's a huge positive. I think that goes with his intelligence and being able to recall things."

Saturday watched for years as Manning was the most mentally prepared player on the field each week. And although Saturday played just one season with Rodgers, he notes the parallels between the two quarterbacks are uncanny. "I think any time you get around people who excel in the quarterback position, those guys learn so much from seeing things and being involved in things and they can recall what hash they're on, what the down and distance were, all that stuff," Saturday said. "And any time you can recall back to plays or blitzes or even formations where they give away tendencies or tips, any time you can recall back to those it gives you a true advantage."

When Rodgers gets to the line of scrimmage, he goes into total recall mode. He remembers what the Bears like to do on third-and-8. He knows what the Lions will do with their safeties against three-wide-receiver looks. And he's pretty sure whether or not the Vikings are disguising a blitz or actually dropping into coverage.

"I've been visualizing since I was in junior high playing sports," Rodgers said. "And I think that approach forces you to be able to recall things very quickly. And you add that to an already pretty good memory. When you visualize, you have to remember those plays that you think about in your mind. So it's stuff that you've seen on tape or plays that you've made in practice. I know my memory is probably not real normal. But I think it's important to have that kind of recall as a quarterback because the ability to react quickly and not be bogged down with your thoughts is an important part of playing the position well.

"I always like to have a picture in my mind as we break the huddle once the play comes in, just a quick recall. It could even be a game I didn't play in where I saw something with that player, something I saw in practice, something I saw on film in that situation. The ability to recall has been a big part of my success, and I think it's something you really need to work on. It's the visualization and the practice of visualization."

As the 2012 season began, Rodgers and the Packers were visualizing big things. The 2011 regular

> ## "I THINK EVERYBODY WOULD BE HAPPY WITH 15–1 DURING THE REGULAR SEASON, BUT AS WE ALL KNOW, THE POSTSEASON IS WHAT COUNTS."
> **—Mike McCarthy**

season had been sublime. The postseason was a nightmare, though. And Rodgers and the Packers were eager to make amends. "It's the goal to be a better team this year, regardless of the record, and the goal is to win the Super Bowl," Packers coach Mike McCarthy said. "I think everybody would be happy with 15–1 during the regular season, but as we all know, the postseason is what counts."

Unlike 2011, though, the Packers started extremely slow.

Green Bay dropped three of its first five games and put itself in an early hole. The Packers lost their home opener to San Francisco, dropped a memorable *Monday Night Football* game in Seattle on a controversial Hail Mary pass that ended the contest, and wasted an 18-point lead at Indianapolis, eventually losing 30–27. Green Bay lost running back Cedric Benson (ankle) for the season against the Colts. And the Packers' already suspect running game became downright putrid.

The Packers—Super Bowl champions just 20 months earlier—were now 2–3 and two games behind division co-leaders Chicago and Minnesota. "We've got the ability, but we're playing bad football," defensive end Ryan Pickett said. "We play well in spots and then we just die. We're not a good team."

The last three times the Packers started 2–3 or worse, they finished 6–10, 8–8, and 4–12. Their season was clearly at a crossroads as they headed to Houston, which had the NFL's best record at 5-0. Throughout the week, many pundits were writing Green Bay's obituary for the 2012 season. Many were also hailing the Texans as the NFL's best team.

Then Rodgers set a career high and tied a franchise record with six touchdown passes, and the Packers beat previously unbeaten Houston 42–24. Jordy Nelson caught three touchdown passes, and James Jones hauled in two.

Rodgers threw for 338 yards and completed 24 of 37 passes. He also tied Matt Flynn's franchise record of six touchdown passes in a game. "This is just a team that has a lot of pride in our locker room," Rodgers said. "I said it this week, there is not a lot of quit in that locker room. It's almost better when people are doubting us a little bit, I think we kind of band together. People tried to pull us apart this week, and we stuck together and found our motivation within."

Rodgers entered the game with a 68.6 completion percentage, 10 touchdown passes, and a 96.9 passer rating. His numbers were solid, but far from his MVP level of 2011. Green Bay's offense ranked just 21st in the NFL after five weeks. And Rodgers had been sacked an astonishing 21 times.

After the victory over Houston, during an on-field interview with NBC, Rodgers was asked what he told the critics. Rodgers, typically the most confident person in whatever room he enters, simply said, "Shhhhh," before walking away.

Later, Rodgers expounded.

"Of course I heard it," Rodgers said of the criticism. "I mean, it wasn't like I paid a lot of attention to it, but people, whether it's good stuff or bad stuff, friends of mine they like to tell me what's being said out there. I'm not someone who watches a lot of TV or puts a whole lot of worth into some of those comments. But I feel like I've always played with a chip on my shoulder, and it helps when people give me a reason to have that chip on my shoulder."

Rodgers certainly played with a chip on his shoulder the rest of the 2012 season. Green Bay won five in a row and nine of its last 11 games that year. Defenses played the Packers differently than past seasons, employing two deep safeties all year and a man underneath, taking away the big play and testing Rodgers' patience. Still, Rodgers stayed within the offense and took what defenses allowed.

That helped the Packers capture the NFC North Division with an 11–5 record, one game better than runners-up Minnesota and Chicago. And Rodgers finished with another huge season. He threw for 39 touchdowns and just eight interceptions, and led the NFL in passer rating (108.0) for a second straight year, becoming the first quarterback to accomplish that since Peyton Manning, who did it from 2004 to 2006. Rodgers finished third in the NFL in completion percentage (67.2), the second-best total in team history behind only his 2011 mark. He also threw for 4,295 yards and led the NFL in touchdown percentage (7.1).

With a big finish, Rodgers vaulted himself back into the MVP discussion again. The award eventually went to Minnesota running back Adrian Peterson, though, who ran for 2,097 yards that season.

"I'm biased," Packers guard T.J. Lang said. "But the way that he plays, I think he's under a big microscope because of how good he is. An average game for him is a really good game for a lot of other people. The way he's had to adjust to how defenses are playing us and still putting up good numbers says a lot about the type of guy he is. I'm always going to say he's the MVP."

Once again, though, the playoffs were a major downer for Green Bay.

The Packers rolled past Minnesota 24–10 in the NFC wild-card round. The Vikings played without starting quarterback Christian Ponder (triceps) and were forced to turn to backup Joe Webb. And the dropoff in ability between the two quarterbacks was precipitous. Rodgers threw for 274 yards and one touchdown, while Webb was just 11-of-30 for 180 yards with one TD and one interception.

"I look at it as I'm going against the Minnesota Vikings' defense, and that's what I've prepared for and that's the film I watched," Rodgers said. "Our defense did a good job today of slowing them down in the passing game and not letting Adrian (Peterson) have the big runs. Joe (Webb) had some good runs early that kept some drives going, but eventually we were able to get ahead and make them have to do some more passing and we did a good job against that."

That set up a homecoming for Rodgers, as the Packers made their way to San Francisco for the NFC Divisional Playoff. Rodgers, who grew up less than three hours north in Chico, California, was headed back to Candlestick Park—where he idolized Joe Montana and Steve Young as a child—for the first time in his NFL career. "It will be fun," Rodgers said. "I went to a few baseball games there growing up, and saw a game there when I was in college. It will be loud, it will be a great environment, and it should be a good show for the fans."

Since the start of the 1995 season, Green Bay was a remarkable 13–2 against the 49ers. The only losses came in the 1998 postseason and the 2012 season opener, in which the 49ers dominated the Packers 30–22 at Lambeau Field.

Rodgers was now presented a chance to leave his mark on a rivalry that was largely one-sided in recent seasons. "I know Aaron Rodgers clearly understands the importance of quarterback play in a game, and more importantly in playoff games," Packers coach Mike McCarthy said. "I know he'll particularly be excited to go back to San Francisco and play in Northern California. That's always exciting for him personally. He's steady. He's been through enough now, I don't see him overreacting or trying to put more pressure on

himself. He's a big-time preparation player as far as what he puts into each game, and that won't change this week. He'll be clutch for us like he always is."

Rodgers was fine against mighty San Francisco. But Green Bay's defense was miserable.

The Packers allowed San Francisco quarterback Colin Kaepernick to account for 444 total yards—including 181 on the ground—and the 49ers cruised to a 45–31 win. Kaepernick also threw for two touchdowns and ran for two more. In all, Green Bay's defense gave up the most total yards (579), yards rushing (323), and second-most points in the playoffs in franchise history

"We just didn't get it done in the second half," Rodgers said. "I knew we were going to have to score some points. We knew we were going to have to put up at least 38 points."

They couldn't. And another season in tiny Green Bay fell short of the ultimate goal. ∎

Though Aaron Rodgers played well against San Francisco in their Divisional Playoff Game at Candlestick Park, the Packers defense could not contain the 49ers offense led by Colin Kaepernick, and fell 45–31.

2013: A MEMORABLE COMEBACK

The 2013 season was a frustrating one for Rodgers and the Packers.

Green Bay dropped two of its first three games for a second consecutive season but then rolled off four straight wins. The Packers averaged 29.0 points per game during their winning streak, and the defense was beginning to take shape.

But on Green Bay's first series during a *Monday Night Football* matchup against Chicago, Rodgers was sacked by Bears defensive end Shea McClellin and broke his collarbone. The injury bug had hit the Packers harder than any team in football since 2010. But this marked the first time Rodgers missed any significant time.

"Aaron's the one guy we really just couldn't lose," Packers veteran cornerback Jarrett Bush said. "We've had a lot of injuries around here, but never really the quarterback. We've been really lucky. But losing Aaron, that's going to be tough."

The Packers had been extremely fortunate when it came to the health of their quarterbacks for more than two decades.

Between 1992 and 2007, ironman Brett Favre made 275 consecutive starts (including playoffs). Of all the records Favre set during his Hall of Fame, 20-year career, his consecutive starts streak—which eventually ended at 321—is likely to stand the longest.

Then, during Rodgers' first five and a half seasons, he missed just one start—due to a concussion in 2010.

Needless to say, the broken collarbone was remarkably frustrating for Rodgers and the Packers.

"It's a difficult injury because there's not a specific type of rehab you can do for this," Rodgers said. "It's not like you can get a massage or stim or the different various treatments that they have out there that can try to get you back quicker. You just have to wait for the bone to heal. That's going to be the frustrating part, but I feel like I've been a quick healer in the past and am hopeful this will be on the short end of whatever prognosis comes up."

The Packers lost that night to Chicago, 27–20. Rodgers would miss the next seven games, too, and Green Bay went just 2–4–1 in those contests. Reserves Seneca Wallace, Scott Tolzien, and eventually Matt Flynn did what they could. But the gap between that trio and Rodgers was enormous—and the Packers slipped to 7–7–1 overall. Green Bay was lost without Rodgers, and not just offensively. When the defense was forced to play more snaps and more minutes, it wilted, too.

Rodgers left Green Bay's Week 9 loss to Chicago after just 2 minutes, 36 seconds. From that moment until Rodgers' return in Week 17, the Packers played 492 minutes, 24 seconds. In that time, Green Bay led for just 81:35—or 16.56 percent of the time.

"We've proven in the past we can lose a lot of guys around here," Packers cornerback Jarrett Bush said. "But A-Rod is different. You can't lose guys like him."

Aaron Rodgers reacts after throwing a go-ahead touchdown pass to wide receiver Randall Cobb with 46 seconds remaining in the Packers' final game of the season, against the Chicago Bears at Soldier Field. The 48-yard score vaulted Green Bay into the playoffs after a frustrating season.

Amazingly, though, as Green Bay headed to the final week of 2013, it still had a chance to win a third straight NFC North title. That's because Detroit had bottomed out and Chicago couldn't pull away inside the extremely mediocre NFC North.

And in the nick of time, Rodgers returned for the regular season finale in Chicago.

"I'm excited to be back with the team," Rodgers said on the day he was cleared by Green Bay's medical staff. "I mean, this is a fun day for me, but I think the focus needs to be on this game and the opportunity we have to win the division, which is our first goal every year. We're in it, you know we have a chance against our rivals, and what better way than to go down there and get some redemption and host a home playoff game."

Late in the game, though, redemption looked highly unlikely.

Green Bay trailed Chicago 28–27, with 46 seconds left in a showdown for the NFC North title—and the division's lone playoff berth. The Packers faced a fourth-and-8 from Chicago's 48-yard line, which in essence meant it was a win-or-go-home play.

The Bears rushed seven, and the Packers blocked with just six. Rodgers was nearly leveled by Bears right end Julius Peppers, but fullback John Kuhn got just enough of Peppers, and Rodgers escaped to his left.

Downfield, Bears safety Chris Conte let wideout Randall Cobb slip behind him. And when Rodgers delivered a strike to Cobb, the shifty receiver raced home for a 48-yard touchdown that gave the Packers a stunning 33–28 win.

It was arguably Green Bay's biggest play in the closing moments of a must-win game since Brett Favre hit Sterling Sharpe for a 40-yard touchdown in the 1993 wild-card game.

"Aaron and Randall just made a phenomenal play," McCarthy said. "Those two guys made a great, great play that will be running on the highlight reel for the rest of my time on this earth. What a great finish."

The play gave Green Bay (8–7–1) a third straight NFC North championship and its seventh divisional

title since 2002. It also vaulted the Packers into the postseason for a fifth straight year under Rodgers.

"I was able to get the edge and saw Randall running wide open," Rodgers said. "I knew I had to get a little bit on it just to make sure that I didn't way under-throw him. When that ball came down in the end zone, it was just pandemonium."

The final play capped a memorable 15-play, 86-yard drive that took nearly six minutes. Along the way, the Packers converted three fourth-down plays. "To pick up three fourth downs on that last drive. Wow," Packers nose tackle Ryan Pickett said. "What are the odds of that?"

Really, the odds of Green Bay's final offensive play working didn't appear great—at least initially. Kuhn, who was serving as Rodgers' personal protector, recognized that the Bears were bringing more rushers than Green Bay had blockers. So Kuhn changed the blocking scheme, making the front five in essence a wall.

Kuhn was then responsible for Peppers, who was coming off the edge. Kuhn was able to get his right shoulder into Peppers' left hip, which did just enough to slow the Bears' pass rusher. "The line did a good job sealing everybody off, leaving one for me," Kuhn said. "I just tried to get as much of [Julius] Peppers as I could."

Rodgers had a rough start to this showdown game with two first half interceptions and a quarterback rating of just 44.7 at halftime. And the Packers were in a 28–20 hole early in the fourth quarter. Back came Rodgers, though, who entered the day with just five fourth quarter comebacks in his career. But Rodgers picked the perfect time for No. 6. First, Rodgers threw for 68 yards during a six-play, 77-yard TD march that pulled the Packers to within a point, at 28–27. Then after the defense came up with its first stop of the second half, Rodgers orchestrated what was arguably the drive of his life.

"It was a special moment," Rodgers said. "There's nothing quite like a road victory and especially on this stage right here. We had to win to get in, otherwise

we're going home. And there were a lot of opportunities for us to give up, and we just kept believing in each other.

"So I'm proud of our guys, thankful for the opportunity. I feel very blessed, I appreciate the prayers from all the fans and obviously my friends and family, but this is a great group of guys. We just want to keep this journey going."

Unfortunately for the Packers, the journey ended one week later.

San Francisco, the defending NFC champs, knocked Green Bay out of the playoffs for a second straight year. Once again, the Packers struggled to contain Kaepernick, and the visiting 49ers edged Green Bay 23–20.

"Yeah, I mean, it's frustrating," Rodgers said afterward. "I think you have to start with yourself and…I could have definitely made a few more plays. So that's why it's disappointing. These opportunities are pretty special, and you've got to make the most of them. It's nine years for me now, blessed to play that long, and would love to play another nine if possible, but this is an opportunity we let slip through our fingers."

Rodgers certainly wasn't at his best against the 49ers. He finished 17-of-26 for 177 yards, with one touchdown and a passer rating of 97.8. Rodgers and the entire offense struggled early, never could get in complete rhythm, and fell to the 49ers for a fourth consecutive time.

"Frustrating way to end the season," Rodgers said. "I think a lot of us felt that the way things had gone the last four or five weeks, there was something special about this year and this might be everything aligning right for us to make a run. So, very disappointing."

The finish ended a wild year for Rodgers, who missed 55 days with his broken collarbone and endured the most frustrating season of his career. Rodgers believed Green Bay had enough talent to make a deep postseason run. Instead, Rodgers and the Packers fell to 1–3 in the playoffs since their Super Bowl season of 2010.

"We did some great things this year," Rodgers said, "but we came up a little short." ■

Aaron Rodgers returned from a broken collarbone suffered in Week 9 versus Chicago for the regular season finale against the team that had knocked him out of action. After a rough start, he completed a stunning comeback that knocked the Bears out of the playoffs and the Packers in.

2014: ONE STEP CLOSER

Life at 30. In the National Football League, that often means the end is near for many players. Running backs are on their last legs. Linemen are breaking down. Cornerbacks and wideouts have lost a step.

When it comes to quarterbacks, though, it's just the opposite.

In the first 49 Super Bowls, exactly half of the quarterbacks to play in the big game were at least 30 years old. Twenty-four of the 49 winning quarterbacks were at least 30 (48.98%), while 25 of the winning quarterbacks had yet to hit the Big 3-0 (51.02%). The average age of all Super Bowl–participating quarterbacks is 29.83—with an average age of 29.69 for the winners and 29.98 for the losers.

So, as the Green Bay Packers saw Rodgers wave good-bye to his twenties in December 2013, there was still plenty of reason to hope. And as the 2014 season began, the 30-year-old Rodgers was excited to follow the path previously blazed by "graybeard" quarterbacks of yesterday.

"This is Titletown," said Rodgers, who was 27 when the Packers won Super Bowl XLV. "This is why they pay us the way the pay us, and there's expectations to win and win now. We feel it, as an older player you feel it even more."

That was understandable. While the window still appeared wide open for Rodgers and the Packers, history showed that would soon begin to change. At the start of the 2014 season, a quarterback 35 years or older had reached the Super Bowl only nine times. And the only ones to win at that advanced age were Denver's John Elway (38 and 37), Baltimore's Johnny Unitas (37), Oakland's Jim Plunkett (36), and Dallas' Roger Staubach (35), until New England's Tom Brady (37) became the latest to do it in Super Bowl XLIX.

So there's no question that the Packers and Rodgers felt a greater sense of urgency heading into 2014. "You sense the hunger that we have, which is exciting," Rodgers said. "The locker room is a little louder than maybe it's been in the last few years, and I think that's just an influx of energy that we have and a general excitement for what we're doing."

Rodgers was just excited to be back and fully healthy from a broken collarbone that sidelined him for nearly half of the 2013 campaign. The Packers had gone 6–2 when Rodgers played a full game in 2013 and 2–5–1 without him. Rodgers was 0–2, though, against archnemesis San Francisco, pushing his losing streak against the 49ers to four games.

By far, the greatest key to the Packers' eventual success or failure in 2014 would be Rodgers' health. Rodgers lost 11 pounds in the offseason, which put his playing weight for the 2014 campaign at 215 pounds. He also began doing yoga to improve his flexibility. "There were some things I shied away from, some heavy lifting, especially shoulder stuff in the offseason,"

Aaron Rodgers led the Packers past the Dallas Cowboys 26–21 in the 2014 NFC Divisional Playoff Game in Green Bay, despite a calf injury.

> ## R-E-L-A-X.....IT'S A LONG SEASON, AND AT SOME POINT WE ARE GOING TO GET THIS THING FIGURED OUT. —Aaron Rodgers

Rodgers said. "But I did my rehab and took it slow and feel good."

Packers coach Mike McCarthy liked what he saw of Rodgers that spring. "I think Aaron's had probably his best spring if I'm going to sit back and try to rank them," McCarthy said. "I'll probably say the same thing next year, but I think he's in great shape. I think Aaron's in a great place and had a very exceptional spring."

Life at 30 can be terrific. And Rodgers couldn't wait to begin proving exactly that.

"Great opportunity for us," Rodgers said of the 2014 season. "It's a combination of team chemistry and staying healthy and then playing the right way at the right time. That's what we did in 2010, and we have to get back there."

The Packers started slowly, much as they had in both 2012 and 2013. Green Bay lost two of its first three games before Rodgers and the offense got rolling in a 38–17 dismantling of host Chicago in Week 4.

Rodgers completed 22 of 28 passes for 302 yards and four touchdowns that afternoon at Soldier Field. Rodgers' final passer rating of 151.2 was the fourth-highest in franchise history, and he averaged a remarkable 10.79 passing yards per attempt.

Just one week earlier, Rodgers and Green Bay's offense managed only seven points in an embarrassing loss at Detroit. Two days after that setback, Rodgers told Packer Nation to "R-E-L-A-X." Then he delivered one of the better games of his career in Chicago.

"I just know it's a long season," Rodgers said. "There's always going to be mini-freakouts along the way. [We] just have to stick together and stay the course. I just wanted to remind everyone that it's a long season, and at some point we are going to get this thing figured out."

Rodgers seemed to have the psyche of these Packers—and really all of Packer Nation—figured out. Instead of making a mountain out of Green Bay's early-season struggles, he settled everyone down with his message to "R-E-L-A-X."

The Packers responded with their best performance of the season, one that started a four-game winning streak. "As a quarterback, you can get too much credit and too much blame at times," Rodgers said. "When you are getting too much credit, you need to be able to deflect properly, and when you are getting too much blame sometimes, you need to tell everyone to relax or just take it all and lead by example when you get on the field."

The Packers followed that with wins over Minnesota, Miami, and Carolina and went to the bye week with a 5–3 record. Rodgers then went wild against the Bears for the second time in 2014.

Rodgers had an unforgettable performance on Sunday Night Football, joining Oakland's Daryle Lamonica as the only players in NFL history to throw six first half touchdown passes. In the first half alone, Rodgers went a remarkable 18-of-24 with six TD strikes, 315 passing yards, and a nearly perfect quarterback rating of 156.3. He needed just seven possessions—and 36 offensive plays—to notch his accomplishment and power the Packers to a remarkably easy 55–14 rout of Chicago.

In a matter of three hours, Rodgers shined before a national audience, became a leading candidate for MVP honors and showed that the Packers might be a legitimate contender in the NFC. "He's just having probably a career year for him," guard T.J. Lang said. "He's been putting up touchdowns, but he's also a guy who doesn't turn the ball over a whole lot. I've seen so many great performances by him that I don't think anything really surprises me anymore. Obviously, that's a little bit unprecedented, though, to have six touchdown passes in the first half."

To say the least.

Lamonica threw six touchdowns in the first half against Buffalo on October 19, 1969. In the 45 years since, no player had notched a six-pack by halftime—until Rodgers destroyed the Bears' atrocious defense.

Packers coach Mike McCarthy was asked afterward if he's ever seen Rodgers better. "I'm going to have to wait until I'm sitting on that porch thinking back," McCarthy said. "But, I mean, he was right on tonight. His statistics at halftime, I don't know if I've ever seen anything like that. He played a great game."

Rodgers had plenty of those during a memorable 2014 campaign. He and the Packers rolled up 53 points during a rout of Philadelphia the following week. That marked the first time in franchise history that Green Bay scored 50 points in consecutive games and just the fifth time in NFL history that a team accomplished the feat.

Rodgers threw a pair of touchdowns in a highly impressive 26–21 home win over eventual Super Bowl–champion New England. And Rodgers threw for 327 yards and three touchdowns in a 43–37 win over Atlanta.

But perhaps his most impressive performance came in the regular season finale against Detroit. With the NFC North title on the line, Rodgers reinjured his left calf late in the first half and took a cart to the Packers' locker room. In the blink of an eye, Detroit turned a 14–0 deficit into a 14-all tie.

But with the Packers on the ropes, Rodgers returned and rallied Green Bay to a 30–20 win. Rodgers engineered touchdown drives on two of his first four second-half possessions and completed 11-of-13 passes for 129 yards.

Green Bay finished the regular season 12–4 and earned the NFC's No. 2 playoff seed and a first-round bye. The Packers also won the NFC North for a fourth straight year. The Lions fell to 11–5 and settled for a wild-card spot.

"I wanted to be back out there, compete with my guys," Rodgers said. "When I broke my collarbone [in 2013], I remember hearing Jon Gruden say that I was out for the game, and I said, 'The hell with that.' [I] tried to get my pads back on and get back out there, but that didn't work obviously with the severity of that injury.

"This was different. Doc [McKenzie] came in, we talked about the risks, and I was able to get him to allow me to do some movements on the sideline to see how I felt. I wasn't going to put myself in major harm's way, but at the same time, I feel like if I can be out there, I can give our team a little jolt....I felt good on the sideline throwing the ball, talked to Mike [McCarthy], asked him to just keep me in the shotgun because of my limited mobility, obviously, and we were able to do that and make some plays."

The Packers finished the year with an NFL-best 486 points, the second-highest total in franchise history. Rodgers was also historically good in games played at Lambeau Field. On his home field, Rodgers threw 25 touchdowns with no interceptions on 240 attempts. Rodgers joined New England quarterback Tom Brady (241 attempts in 2003) as the only other quarterback in NFL history with 200-plus pass attempts at home in a season without an interception.

Rodgers recorded a passer rating of 133.2 at home during the 2014 regular season, the highest in NFL history. And the Packers outscored their foes by an NFL-best 155 points in eight home games, the highest-mark in franchise history.

"Right now, I'd say it's going to be tough for someone to beat us here," Packers cornerback Tramon Williams said of Green Bay's homefield advantage. "We haven't played like this ever. We've played well, but not like this. If we are playing like this at home, then obviously people probably won't want to come here. It's not going to be easy at all, but it's pretty great how we're playing right now."

Green Bay opened the postseason by hosting longtime rival Dallas in the NFC Divisional Playoff. And with Rodgers limited by his calf injury, the Packers were in a 21–13 hole late in the third quarter. But with the season on the line, Rodgers scrapped the conservative nature he played with for three quarters and turned it loose down the stretch.

First, Rodgers engineered a seven-play, 90-yard TD march that pulled the Packers to within a point, 21–20. Rodgers fired a 46-yard touchdown to rookie wideout Davante Adams on a third-and-15, as the rookie wideout beat Sterling Moore and J.J. Wilcox for the score.

One series later, Rodgers led an eight-play, 80-yard scoring drive in which 78 of the yards came via Rodgers' right arm. Rodgers capped the march with a 13-yard bullet TD to rookie tight end Richard Rodgers that gave Green Bay a lead it wouldn't relinquish.

The Packers prevailed and headed to their second NFC Championship Game under Rodgers.

"Just an incredible effort by [Rodgers], especially in the second half to go out there and grind and continue to make plays when he's not 100 percent healthy," Lang said. "But he's our leader, and everything starts with him."

The Packers headed to Seattle for the NFC Championship Game. The defending Super Bowl–champion Seahawks had routed the Packers 36–16 in the season opener and were a 7.5-point favorite in the rematch.

For most of the game, though, the Packers dominated the mighty Seahawks.

Green Bay held a 16–0 halftime lead. And according to ProFootballReference.com, the Packers' chances of winning at that point were 94.4 percent. Green Bay also led 19–7 with just over three minutes left in the game. And at that moment, the Packers' chances of winning were 99.9 percent.

Aaron Rodgers targets Randall Cobb (18) for a pass during the first half of the NFC Championship Game against the Seattle Seahawks.

But somehow, someway, the Seahawks rallied for the most improbable 28–22 win in overtime.

Green Bay's offense became conservative and predictable. The defense melted down. And Packers' reserve tight end Brandon Bostick fumbled away Seattle's onside kick that could have iced the game.

In overtime, Seahawks wideout Jermaine Kearse beat Packers cornerback Tramon Williams for a 35-yard, game-winning touchdown when the Packers blitzed and had no safety help. "I tried to watch the film…but I didn't," Packers left guard Josh Sitton said. "I couldn't watch it. I knew what happened. We kicked their ass up front, and the whole game. We handled them all day. We should've won the game."

Rodgers wasn't his typical self due to both the calf injury and Seattle's elite defense. Rodgers finished with two interceptions, one touchdown, and a 55.8 passer rating. It marked his second disappointing individual performance in an NFC Championship Game.

But Green Bay was in control virtually the entire game. And afterward, everyone agreed that a golden opportunity was wasted. "It's a missed opportunity that I will probably think about the rest of my career," Rodgers said. "We were the better team…and we played well enough to win, and we can't blame anybody but ourselves."

Despite the brutal loss, Rodgers had arguably the best season of his career and won his second MVP in four years. Rodgers completed 341 of 520 passes (65.6 percent) for 4,381 yards and 38 TDs. He also threw just five interceptions and finished with a 112.2 passer rating.

Rodgers again ranked No. 1 in touchdown-to-interception ratio (38-to-5, or 7.60) and finished second in the NFL in passer rating and yards-per-attempt (8.43). Rodgers was third in touchdown passes and was the only quarterback in the NFL to finish in the top three in all four of those categories.

"I need to figure out new ways to compliment Aaron, frankly," McCarthy said.

While the ending to the 2014 season was heartbreaking, the first half of Rodgers' career has been remarkable. In addition to a Super Bowl title and two MVP awards, Rodgers has led the Packers to six straight playoff appearances.

Rodgers and the Packers have won four straight NFC North Division titles, something that hadn't been done since Chicago won five in a row in the mid-1980s. And Rodgers has compiled a 70–33 record in the regular season (.680) and is 6–5 in the postseason (.545).

To think, Rodgers nearly gave the game up as an 18-year-old back in Chico, California. And as recently as 2009, a large segment of the fan base wanted to move on from the trio of Rodgers, McCarthy, and Thompson.

"We've all gained a lot by working together," Rodgers said. "All relationships that last are built on trust. And trust for me is not initially given. It's earned. And Mike's the same way. I'm kind of a laid-back, California guy. He's a loud Pittsburgh guy. So it took a while to get on the same page, I think, as far as our styles meshing together. But the thing that always helped was the preparation we always put in and how much we desired to be successful, and it was only a matter of time before things started clicking the right way."

As the 2015 season dawned, Rodgers was already part of an elite club of just 31 men who have been a Super Bowl–winning quarterback. But only 11 quarterbacks have won multiple Super Bowl championships.

Terry Bradshaw, Joe Montana, and Tom Brady all won four Super Bowls. Troy Aikman won three, while Bart Starr, Roger Staubach, Bob Griese, Jim Plunkett, John Elway, Ben Roethlisberger, and Eli Manning have won two apiece.

Rodgers would like nothing more than to someday become the 12th member of that prestigious club.

"The numbers are great. The stats are great because it means you've done some terrific things as an offense," Rodgers said. "But you're remembered by championships. I get that."

The chase for greatness continues. ∎